Racism

Other Books in the Social Issues Firsthand Series:

SOCIAL ISSUES
FIRSTHAND

Racism

Hayley Mitchell Haugen, Book Editor

GREENHAVEN PRESS
A part of Gale, Cengage Learning

GALE
CENGAGE Learning·

Detroit • New York • San Francisco • New Haven, Conn • Waterville, Maine • London

GALE
CENGAGE Learning

Christine Nasso, *Publisher*
Elizabeth Des Chenes, *Managing Editor*

© 2008 Greenhaven Press, a part of Gale Cengage Learning.

For more information, contact:
Greenhaven Press
27500 Drake Rd.
Farmington Hills, MI 48331-3535
Or you can visit our Internet site at http://www.gale.com

LIBRARY OF CONGRESS CATALOGING-IN-PUBLICATION DATA

Racism / Hayley Mitchell Haugen, book editor.
    p. cm. -- (Social issues firsthand)
    Includes bibliographical references and index.
    ISBN-13: 978-0-7377-2901-6 (hardcover)
    ISBN-10: 0-7377-2901-5 (hardcover)
    1. Racism--United States--Anecdotes--Juvenile literature. 2. Racism in education --United States--Anecdotes--Juvenile literature. 3. Violence--United States --Anecdotes--Juvenile literature. 4. Minorities--United States--Biography --Anecdotes--Juvenile literature. 5. Immigrants--United States--Biography --Anecdotes--Juvenile literature. 6. United States--Race relations--Anecdotes-- Juvenile literature. 7. Racism--Anecdotes--Juvenile literature. I. Haugen, Hayley Mitchell, 1968-
        E184.A1R3265 2008
        305.800973--dc22
                                                                2007033048

Printed in the United States of America
2 3 4 5 6 7 12 11 10 09 08

Contents

Chapter 3: Racism, Tragedy, and Violence

Foreword

Social issues are often viewed in abstract terms. Pressing challenges such as poverty, homelessness, and addiction are viewed as problems to be defined and solved. Politicians, social scientists, and other experts engage in debates about the extent of the problems, their causes, and how best to remedy them. Often overlooked in these discussions is the human dimension of the issue. Behind every policy debate over poverty, homelessness, and substance abuse, for example, are real people struggling to make ends meet, to survive life on the streets, and to overcome addiction to drugs and alcohol. Their stories are ubiquitous and compelling. They are the stories of everyday people—perhaps your own family members or friends—and yet they rarely influence the debates taking place in state capitols, the national Congress, or the courts.

The disparity between the public debate and private experience of social issues is well illustrated by looking at the topic of poverty. Each year the U.S. Census Bureau establishes a poverty threshold. A household with an income below the threshold is defined as poor, while a household with an income above the threshold is considered able to live on a basic subsistence level. For example, in 2003 a family of two was considered poor if its income was less than $12,015; a family of four was defined as poor if its income was less than $18,810. Based on this system, the bureau estimates that 35.9 million Americans (12.5 percent of the population) lived below the poverty line in 2003, including 12.9 million children below the age of eighteen.

Commentators disagree about what these statistics mean. Social activists insist that the huge number of officially poor Americans translates into human suffering. Even many families that have incomes above the threshold, they maintain, are likely to be struggling to get by. Other commentators insist that the statistics exaggerate the problem of poverty in the United States. Compared to people in developing countries, they point out, most so-called poor families have a high quality of life. As stated by journalist Fidelis Iyebote, "Cars are owned by 70 percent of 'poor' households. . . . Color televisions belong to 97 percent of the 'poor' [and] videocassette recorders belong to nearly 75 percent. . . . Sixty-four percent have microwave ovens, half own a stereo system, and over a quarter possess an automatic dishwasher."

However, this debate over the poverty threshold and what it means is likely irrelevant to a person living in poverty. Simply put, poor people do not need the government to tell them whether they are poor. They can see it in the stack of bills they cannot pay. They are aware of it when they are forced to choose between paying rent or buying food for their children. They become painfully conscious of it when they lose their homes and are forced to live in their cars or on the streets. Indeed, the written stories of poor people define the meaning of poverty more vividly than a government bureaucracy could ever hope to. Narratives composed by the poor describe losing jobs due to injury or mental illness, depict horrific tales of childhood abuse and spousal violence, recount the loss of friends and family members. They evoke the slipping away of social supports and government assistance, the descent into substance abuse and addiction, the harsh realities of life on the streets. These are the perspectives on poverty that are too often omitted from discussions over the extent of the problem and how to solve it.

Greenhaven Press's Social Issues Firsthand series provides a forum for the often-overlooked human perspectives on society's most divisive topics of debate. Each volume focuses on one social issue and presents a collection of ten to sixteen narratives by those who have had personal involvement with the topic. Extra care has been taken to include a diverse range of perspectives. For example, in the volume on adoption, readers will find the stories of birth parents who have made an adoption plan, adoptive parents, and adoptees themselves. After exposure to these varied points of view, the reader will have a clearer understanding that adoption is an intense, emotional experience full of joyous highs and painful lows for all concerned.

The debate surrounding embryonic stem cell research illustrates the moral and ethical pressure that the public brings to bear on the scientific community. However, while nonexperts often criticize scientists for not considering the potential negative impact of their work, ironically the public's reaction against such discoveries can produce harmful results as well. For example, although the outcry against embryonic stem cell research in the United States has resulted in fewer embryos being destroyed, those with Parkinson's, such as actor Michael J. Fox, have argued that prohibiting the development of new stem cell lines ultimately will prevent a timely cure for the disease that is killing Fox and thousands of others.

Each book in the series contains several features that enhance its usefulness, including an in-depth introduction, an annotated table of contents, bibliographies for further research, a list of organizations to contact, and a thorough index. These elements—combined with the poignant voices of people touched by tragedy and triumph—make the Social Issues Firsthand series a valuable resource for research on today's topics of political discussion.

Introduction

When asked to share their experiences with racism, some students are surprised. Many have not encountered racism in their daily lives and do not know others who have been discriminated against because of their race. Racism, to them, is more theoretical than personal, a topic of debate for news anchors and politicians, not a topic of concern among their own family and friends.

Social studies teacher Tom McKenna teaches at a high school in Portland, Oregon. He says that his students call him a racist. "They claim racism doesn't exist in our society," he explains. "Therefore, anyone who brings up race when analyzing injustice is a racist. According to them, I fit the bill."[1] McKenna's students believe that it is easier to be black in America than white. Black students get all the scholarships, they say. And they talk about relatives who they believe lost job opportunities because of affirmative action policies. They do not see that their attitudes have already been influenced by racism. McKenna admits that he and his intern realize "how much work we have to do in order to broaden our students' understanding about issues of race."[2]

Even adults can be lulled into mistakenly thinking that racism is nonexistent where they happen to live and work. Dr. Stephanie Sellers, for example, is a part-time English professor at a small liberal arts college, which she does not name, in central Pennsylvania. As she writes for the *American Indian Quarterly*, when she first arrived on campus, she "foolishly believed racism could not exist at this fine college so lauded for its commitment to civil rights and the highest academic endeavors."[3] After working at the campus for only a short time, however, she discovered that an "ever-widening gulf grew between [her and her colleagues] because of [their] cultural differences."[4] Although she was a highly educated professional,

Sellers felt belittled by her coworkers because of her Native American heritage. They made her feel invisible by not recognizing the importance of her scholarship in Native American history and literature. "They would talk to me like I was an imbecile," she writes, "because my version of history, methodology, and understanding of literature sharply contrasted from theirs."[5] Sellers found that students on her campus also held racist opinions about Native Americans. One referred to the them as "those drunkards who live in shacks and trailers out West,"[6] and another was surprised that Native Americans have their own newspaper.

Racism in the News

McKenna's students' misunderstandings about racism and Sellers' personal experiences with racism in Pennsylvania have certainly gone unnoticed, for the most part, by the rest of America. More public events covered by the American media, however, frequently show that racism is a recurring topic of debate in the United States. For instance, in 2005 Hurricane Katrina destroyed much of New Orleans and other communities along the Gulf Coast. In the aftermath of the storm, President George W. Bush and his administration was widely criticized for their handling of the crisis, when thousands of New Orleans residents remained stranded for days without adequate provisions of food, water, or shelter. *Boston Globe* columnist Cathy Young writes, "Katrina's devastation exposed to a harsh daylight the often ignored problems of the black underclass."[7] Young believes that the "race mongers" took advantage of this exposure to portray President Bush as ambivalent to the fate of African Americans. She reports that white people were just as victimized by government ineptitude as black people, but the media highlighted the racism angle in much of their coverage of and debate about the disaster.

The topic of racism flooded the media again on April 4, 2007, when radio talk-show personality Don Imus referred to the Rutgers University women's basketball team as a bunch of "nappy-headed hos." As a result, CBS fired Imus for his racial slurs. On the heels of the Imus controversy, on April 16, another event sparked discussions of race and racism in America. Twenty-three-year-old Seung-Hui Cho, a student at Virginia Polytechnic Institute and State University (Virginia Tech), went on a shooting spree on campus, killing thirty-two people and injuring fifteen others before taking his own life. The university reported that the shooting was not a hate crime, but the media speculated whether the Korean national's actions were racially motivated.

One Woman's Rage

Hurricane Katrina, the Don Imus episode, and the Virginia Tech shootings are three events that received much attention by the American media. Each raised Americans' awareness about racism by sparking debate about the issue. In addition to the television and print coverage of these events, the personal narratives that have emerged in their wake have expressed the humiliation, loss, and anger that victims of racism feel during these very public displays of discrimination, ignorance, and violence.

While public events keep racism in the news, racism also occurs every day on a smaller, more private scale, outside of media coverage. Bell hooks, an African American author and distinguished professor of English at the City College of New York, writes frequently about her personal experiences with racism. In her essay, "Killing Rage" for example, she analyzes her own rage that has grown out of the many discriminatory attitudes she has faced in her daily life. In one example, hooks admits to feeling a "killing rage" toward a white man on a plane after a day filled with a series of what she describes as "racialized incidents."[8] Hooks is so angry at the man for refusing to move from a first-class seat meant for her friend that she wants to "stab him softly, to shoot him with the gun I wished I had in my purse. And as I watched his pain, I would say to him tenderly, 'racism hurts.'"[9]

Rather than turn to violence, though, hooks turned to writing. She took out a legal pad and analyzed, through writing her essay, her own history of oppression, what she sees as other African Americans' complicity in racism, and how her feelings of rage can contribute to a kind of constructive self-healing. "Confronting my rage," she writes, "witnessing the way it moved me to grow and change, I understood intimately that it had the potential not only to destroy but also to construct."[10]

People like hooks write personal narratives about racism because racism *is* a problem in American society. When published for a broad audience, these personal narratives have the power to change people's perceptions about the state of racism today. Published in 2001, *Writing as Reflective Action* by Sherrie Gradin and Duncan Carter is used by college-level writing instructors nationwide and each year a fresh batch of students encounters the challenging essays of the text, including hooks's volatile essay, "Killing Rage" in the first chapter.

Whether or not students believe that racism is an American problem, the "Reflective Reading" questions at the end of hooks's essay force them to consider the topic from both rhetorical and personal angles. First, students reflect on hooks's personal experience, pinpointing the events that led to her feelings of rage, and they consider how these events are connected to social class and economics. Other questions about hooks's audience, her choice of vocabulary, and her use of anecdotes are included as well.

Ultimately, though, these questions lead up to a writing assignment option at the end of the chapter that asks students to write their own race-based essay. They are encouraged to "re-see" their own class and race in light of hooks's essay, to consider whether they have ever been victims of racism themselves or whether, perhaps, they have been part of the problem. Although these student narratives generally go unpublished, they do keep the conversation about racism alive, reminding students that there are real people behind this often politicized topic.

Notes

1. Tom McKenna, "Confronting Racism, Promoting Respect: A Union Program Tackles a Difficult Topic," Rethinking Schools Online, Summer 1999, www.rethinkingschoolsonline.org.
2. McKenna, "Confronting Racism, Promoting Respect."
3. Stephanie Sellers, "The Experience of a Native American English Professor in Central Pennsylvania," *American Indian Quarterly* 27, no. 1–2 (Winter–Spring 2003): 412–415.
4. Sellers, "The Experience of a Native American English Professor."
5. Sellers, "The Experience of a Native American English Professor."
6. Sellers, "The Experience of a Native American English Professor."
7. Cathy Young, "No. This Is the Story of the Hurricane," *Reason*, December 2005, pp. 19–21.
8. bell hooks, "Killing Rage," in *Writing as Reflective Action*, by Sherrie Gradin and Duncan Carter, New York: Longman, 2001, pp. 102–11.
9. hooks, "Killing Rage."
10. hooks, "Killing Rage."

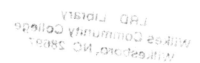

SOCIAL ISSUES
FIRSTHAND

CHAPTER 1

Everyday Racism

Covert Racism Is Everywhere

Nadine McNeil

Nadine McNeil is a Jamaican-born British freelance writer, who describes herself as a "visionary writer and storyteller." In the following article, she reflects on people's unwillingness to discuss matters of race, despite various atrocities that have taken place because of racism. McNeil describes the racial injustice emerging out of the diamond trade in Africa as well as the racism that stems from white supremacy in the United States. She warns that unless people of all races begin to talk about race, their voices will go unheard forever and racial inequality will continue.

A recurring question for me prompts this discourse: what am I? Female, black, both or neither? Seemingly, the answer is obvious. But is it really?

When I enter a room, what does one see "first," my race or my gender? My initial response is that I am identified and oftentimes subsequently defined by the color of my skin.

Another frequent observation is the unwillingness by human beings to openly discuss the issue of race amongst ourselves as well as across borders. For example, it has been my experience that black folk of the lighter persuasion are reluctant to admit the "one uppance" that a "li'l milk" gives them. Is this due to the illusion of white privilege and the taste of power that is "enjoyed" as a consequence? Or is it because this enjoyment is complex and bittersweet given that the very lightness that they may enjoy in one community of which they are a product is rejected in another of which they are also part and parcel?

When I have attempted to engage white folk in a discussion about race, the "reflex reaction" is one of appalling defense—"I wasn't around when slavery was taking place so why should I now be held responsible?" In the words of Joy DuGry Leary, author of *Post Traumatic Slavery Syndrome*, "[do] you think *I* was?"

Healing Comes Through Sharing

In recent times, I have been afforded the position of witnessing leaders (all male) from first world nations echoing apologies for the slave trade and even a few leaders mentioned the holocaustic intergenerational aftermath. Again the victim (most often female and a person of color) or the victim's children's children are forced to forgive with the ultimatum: If humanity is to move forward then we have little alternative but to believe that their apologies are heartfelt and sincere. Rather than resolve, doesn't this "gloss over" and further perpetuate the slave mentality and victim-hood?

Viewing my black sisters in Sierra Leone whose limbs and ears were sliced off by insurgents, rebels' forced pregnancy and rape a normal occurrence, and their off-spring doped up into being child soldiers, their perpetrators were given amnesty and vocational training while the women, victims of cruel and inhumane atrocities languished in poverty in their enforced forgiveness campaign by the Sierra Leone government.

These abhorrent acts were carried out so that "lovely little white girls" [in America and elsewhere] could wear diamond rings. At the same time the origin of diamonds excavated from African soil do not grace women of color due to poverty, slavery and violence perpetrated over Africa's natural resource. In this era of [so-called] civilisation, Belgian colonizers rape the African land of her jewels and the people of their dignity all for their own greed.

Only we—the Black Diaspora—can release our ancestral shame if we are to heal our intergenerational trauma and wounds caused by being enslaved. The first step in this release comes from sharing—amongst ourselves and along with others.

Healing occurs once we have embraced the hurt, the anger, the rejection, the brutality, the disappointment, the rape, the murders and the lynchings. Facing reality such as these overt actions through many centuries which continue to be covertly dumped in present day is a necessary brutality and life experience within the Black Diaspora.

Covert Racism Is Everywhere, and Where You Least Expect It

Through the brutal reality of my own Black Jamaican female life experiences I recognized my yearnings and longings are a path and creed from which to propel away from black slavery, not to entrench the slave/victim mentality.

I long for the day when I am able to enter a bank and not be thrown "off center" by a clerk perhaps with less than a quarter of my educational background and professional experience treating me as though I am her subordinate.

I long for the day that when I show my credentials on paper, I am not forced to bear witness in person to their discomfort because my profile doesn't match their stereotype.

I long for the day when I board an aircraft and "coincidentally" find that all people of colour have been seated in a defined area within the aircraft. I long for the day when, "a colour of a [person's] skin is of no more significance than the colour of his eyes. And until the basic human rights are equally guaranteed to all without regard to race . . . And until that day, a world of lasting peace will remain but a fleeting illusion to be pursued but never attained." ("War," written by H.I.M. Emperor Haile Selassie, disseminated by Universal Legend, Bob Marley.)

What's worse about covert racism is that when we do choose to voice it as "glaring examples" to our white colleagues, friends, peers, our experiences are frequently invalidated with such comments as: "Are you sure s/he said or did this or that? Perhaps they were having a bad day."

Such comments intended—oftentimes with the best of sincerity—to make us feel better—have the direct opposite effect of patronage and are lethal weapons perpetuating white supremacy. Unconsciousness of their white privilege and entitlement affords a position of "power over" even in these small actions and responses.

Some Racism Stems from White Supremacy

When "whites" describe the Irish as being "the blacks of Europe" at face value the statement is intended to display some sort of empathy for my plight. Unconscious white privilege starts to acknowledge the "power over" hierarchy present in white supremacy that impacts them directly and it is exploitive to expect empathy and any relationship to people of color racial issues.

At a deeper level, relating whites designated as "blacks" is actually insensitive and again stems from white racist supremacy. Unlike me whose ethnicity is abundantly clear upon sight, the Irish are identified and defined only once they open their mouths. For a period, white Irish people are afforded the white privilege and can choose to be immersed in it until they speak.

This further perpetuates racist socialization that endorses me to be someone who I in fact mightn't be; i.e., a [stereo-] typical black female—single mother, with multiple partners, drug addict, prostitute, maid, HIV/AIDS carrier, entertainer, athlete. And given that I represent part of the Diaspora defying this stereotype, "she must be 'super smart!'"

In an intricate exchange with Danica Anderson, executive director, The Kolo: Women's Cross Cultural Collaboration, we candidly shared about the impact of white supremacy. Anderson's work in Bosnia with the frontline women as well as in Africa, India and Sri Lanka prompted her painful look at white supremacy issues.

"Like the issue of gender along socio-cultural lines, the racial divide will not be bridged until humanity is willing to embrace and honor diversity," she strongly feels.

The "white supremacy blindspot" continues to perpetuate, highlighted in the US without meaningful dialogue among blacks and whites about the issue of race, and continues intergenerationally.

Racism Can Be Both Blatant and Subtle

In Jamaica, I was brought up being told we are objects of class prejudice. When I went to live in the United States I experienced racism firsthand. The racism I felt was blatant, yet subtle—like when I'd walk onto the subway and a white person would clutch their purse a tad tighter.

Of her childhood days in Chicago, Anderson recounts that her father, a violent Bosnian patriarch, made so many racist comments about Blacks. "Many of the references were the famous N--- word. I grew up to mouth the hatred against Blacks, Hispanics- Spics who were Puerto Rican and especially the Croatians who, according to my father were responsible for the WWII Genocide of Serbs."

Even where there is solidarity amongst women, there is a fine point at which this "sisterhood" diverges.

"White women are treated differently and differentially. It is mind-boggling how quickly white supremacy rushes past the skin color into the psyche. It is embattled on an overt and covert basis to the point where I as a white female cannot even recognize my privileged life," says Anderson.

White supremacy forges on with ruling leaders irrespective of skin color. Subtle and overt indoctrination driven from a need to be at the top of the white pyramid at the expense of humanity triggers their survivor mechanisms into overdrive, resulting in our modern age super genocidal chapters.

Black men are behind bars at alarming rates and [hetero-sexual] women of color between the ages of 25 and 44 years old are among the fastest growing HIV/AIDS rates in the United States of America. And yet we have failed to engage each other in meaningful dialogue.

Racial paralysis now threatens to render us mute.

Racist Like Me

Debra Dickerson

Debra Dickerson is a lawyer and prolific American essayist who frequently writes on race relations. She has been both a senior editor and a contributing editor at U.S. News & World Report, and her work has also appeared in the New York Times Magazine, the Washington Post, the New Republic, Slate, the Village Voice, and Essence. In the following essay, Dickerson admits that she has internalized hatred of African Americans. Although she is black, she says she has become a racist. She urges victims of racism and other discrimination to come forward to educate others. She muses on the fact that although class warfare makes sense to her, racial warfare is not natural. Acknowledging her own racist tendencies, however, helps stir her compassion for others, and she encourages others to do the same.

In a nation riven to its very core by race, I appear to be the only remaining racist. Off and on, I'm homophobic and anti-Semitic, too, but mostly, I'm racist. Yet unlike the rest of you, I'm honest about it.

I'm the only person I know who routinely admits to being a racist. When I redeemed my Mother's Day spa package, I was assigned a lovely young black woman as my aesthetician. As we chatted, I found myself searching for words. Eventually, I realized I was trying to find a way to ask about her credentials. In 20 years of spa trips, I have never had a black aesthetician, and I have never thought, let alone asked, about one's competence, even when they disappoint me. It appears that I, too, think black people are stupid, uninformed, and graceless. Criminal, too—day before yesterday, after finalizing the details of working in a public housing complex, I dreamt that night of herds of rapacious, animalistic blacks robbing, assaulting, and generally terrorizing me there. (*Birth of a Nation* [a landmark film about the Civil War and Reconstruction as seen through the eyes of white Southerners] was more subtle.) So, counting yesterday's incident, which I will recount shortly, that makes twice just this week that I was a racist.

Victims Can Educate Others

It was yesterday's incident that got me thinking about how racism is lived. The *New York Times* recently won a Pulitzer for a series on how race is lived, but that's not quite the same thing, is it? Most of us agree that racism is far from dead and that we're all responsible for helping to end it. And yet, so charged is the issue of race that it is virtually impossible for those who do not already agree about it to discuss it. Without a free exchange of ideas, progress is not very likely; conservatives will continue to preach to their choir and liberals will do the same.

Here's an example: A gay friend was being cavalier and dismissive, I thought, about the least divergence from the gay agenda, even by a pro-gay person like me. He wouldn't even entertain the notion that, say, lesbians in a women's locker room could legitimately give one pause. It shouldn't be a long pause (given that they've always been there), but give me a break. From the look on his face, you'd have thought that I had said he was going to sodomite hell. "Oh Debra. From you?" I argued that a man would never be allowed into a women's locker room—even if he were physically incapable of either sex or violence (I also made him blind for good measure). My friend sighed deeply, looked to the heavens as if praying for patience, and then grandly "forgave" me by abruptly changing the subject. Clearly, he considered any such discussion homophobic, a designation I escaped solely on the strength of our friendship. But why couldn't we discuss it? The notion that "victim" status exempts him from the need to examine, explain, or defend his beliefs is a dangerous one indeed. That was the perfect moment both to prove to himself that he'd thought things through, and to educate someone who could go forth and spread knowledge. Instead, we just showed each other that you can love and respect someone and yet know that they can sometimes be self-righteous, intolerant, and anti-intellectual.

One reason for bigotry's maddening intractability is that a determination—however kneejerk, superficial, or unthinkingly made—that something or someone is racist ends the discussion, as happened with my friend. The verdict is "guilty" and the only punishment is forfeiture of the right to consider yourself a decent human being. Better to be a necrophiliac than an admitted bigot. Yet if we are to evolve on the issue of race, the notion that you, or someone else, is racist ought to function as the beginning of the attainment of full humanity, not the proof that you've relinquished it. Realizing with each incident that I was operating from a no-longer-quite-subconscious script about race allowed me to recognize, and then confront, the hateful notions I have internalized about blacks. Worse, it allowed me to see that having experienced racism had helped turn me into one: It turns out that I have a problem with whites, too.

Everyday Racism in Action

Yesterday, I watched a white man park his truck in my driveway and walk off down the road without even a glance to see if the owners were about so he could ask permission. The sense of entitlement and ownership he exuded pushed every race-, gender- and class-based button a black girl from the inner city has to push. Guys like that have been pushing the world (read: me) around forever. Still, I tried to shrug it off. Then, when I went out for the mail two hours later, I was furious to see his truck still on my property. In full Gloria Steinem [an American feminist icon] meets Fannie Lou Hamer [an inspirational civil rights activist] mode, I marched down the road to the construction site where I figured he'd gone.

At the site, a gaggle of "Joe College"–type shirtless white boys were goofing off, and a grandfatherly black man half-heartedly directed nonexistent traffic. As I approached, the black man perked up, glad to see me in this extremely white part of an extremely white city in an extremely white region. Or perhaps he was glad because now he wasn't the only adult. The white guys, suddenly busy with their rakes, feigned blindness. "Whose truck—"

The black man strode over and pointed gleefully at the man who was clearly in charge. "The green hat! That's his truck." How had he known what I was going to say? With happy spite, the black man watched as I exchanged a few words with my squatter and saluted me as the man who must be his boss followed me shamefacedly to move his truck. As I passed the brother, I said evilly, "If I'd parked on his property, the police would be here."

"You got that right," he agreed grimly, as if I'd narrowly escaped the noose. It's a wonder we didn't flash each other black power salutes. But the moment the words were out of my mouth, I was ashamed. Worse: I felt stupid.

Who am I kidding? I'm an attorney. The lots are so big in my deer-filled suburb that I had to drive from neighbor to neighbor to collect petition signatures for a local election. In fact, we rarely even use that usurped driveway because we have two. My architect husband is white as are our two children. (So far. Biracial kids often darken over time.) The local police are just as respectful of me as they are of my neighbors, whatever they might be thinking. Whether or not I should fear them, I don't.

It is a testament to the enduring legacy of racism that a black grandfather still doing manual labor bothered to side with either me or my squatter. He should have said to hell with the both of you and played dumb, leaving the two of us to fight over our possessions. I'm guessing he'd also witnessed his feudal lord take arrogant possession of a stranger's property and that this had pushed all his buttons, too. The fact that I turned out to be black was the icing on the cake.

Class Conflict Is Natural

In a way, I'm arguing for class warfare to replace racial warfare. Class conflict makes sense; it keeps the powerful from riding roughshod over senior citizens who can't retire from manual labor in the hot sun. The truth is, I have far more in common with the rich white man than I do with that poor black grandfather (who would never dare to park on private property in this neighborhood). A world of perfect harmony would be lovely, but until the rapture comes I'd rather blue-collar types of all races faced off against us "suits" than one race against the other. There is nothing logical, natural, or beneficial about a world organized by race—the very concept is irrational. Any system divided along racial lines, implicitly or overtly, will be immoral, inefficient, and unstable. (Take, for example, poor whites' hatred of slaves, rather than of slavery, for depressing wages.)

Class conflict, on the other hand, is natural and rational. It brought us the minimum wage, OSHA [Occupational Safety and Health Administration], Social Security, the weekend, overtime, pensions, and the like. While none of those are unmitigated successes, a system organized along class lines acknowledges that capitalism doesn't police itself and that labor must have a voice—it wasn't the capitalists who pushed for child labor laws and the eight-hour work day. Everybody loses when societal goods are distributed on the basis of race, even those in the front of the bus. Bigotry is just plain stupid, but as long as the price of examining one's prejudices is expulsion from the human race, we're never going to be able to quash it.

Acknowledging Racism Stirs Compassion

When I realized that I had internalized the world's loathing of blacks, my first response was, counterintuitively, relief. Finally, I have proof that blacks' obsession with racism isn't crazy. If I secretly think that many poor blacks are animalistic and stupid, you'll never make me believe that lots of other people don't, too. My lasting response has been chagrined amusement to realize that I hold such ridiculous, illogical notions. Most of all, acknowledging my own racism has given me a measure of compassion for how difficult it is to retain one's humanity in such a politicized and inhumane world. I'm black and I make my living thinking about race, but I still wasn't immune to the insidious bigotry in our world. How much harder it must be for those with far less time to contemplate and come to terms with these vexing social issues.

It's not bigotry per se that hamstrings us in the struggle to achieve a just society. It's our inability to talk about and think our way through our preconceptions. We have to learn how to forgive each other, and more importantly ourselves, when we're stupid.

Remaining Positive in the Face of Racism

Stefan Chiarantano

Canadian artist and English instructor Stefan Chiarantano teaches English as a second language to junior high and elementary school students in Japan. In the following article he writes of his experiences with racism in Asia, where the locals have called him names in their native tongues, refused to sit next to him on the bus, and have outwardly shown their resentment of his presence in other ways. Even his students have been rude to him. Despite this mistreatment, Chiarantano refuses to get angry. He delights in the many good friends he has made in Asian cultures, and he focuses on his positive experiences.

This article isn't meant as a critique or a means to denigrate other cultures but simply to share my experiences of living abroad and put them in a context and frame of reference. It's about seeing things in a new light.

I'd been a social worker in Toronto, Canada and had wanted a change of pace and scenery for some time. I was drawn to Asia because of my interest in Buddhism and Asian art and culture. I first taught English in Taiwan and now I'm living and working in Maebashi, Japan.

I'm still at it and enjoy the challenge of teaching at a junior high school and also in two elementary schools. Little things are different, like trading outside shoes for an indoor pair of shoes or runners which are to be worn only inside the school, with yet another pair required to enter the gym. But Japan's incredibly orderly like that. It's a place where cars and pedestrians actually wait for the lights to change before proceeding.

Stefan Chiarantano, "Staying Positive in the Face of Racism," www.familylifeabroad .com, April 17, 2007. Reproduced by permission of the author.

When I went abroad to teach, I didn't expect to be welcomed with open arms but I also hadn't counted on dealing with the constant xenophobic-like behaviour. Here are some of my experiences.

The Japanese Do Not Always Welcome Foreigners

Once, I nearly had to physically restrain a colleague from bashing in the heads of a group of Japanese revelers sitting next to us in a Japanese pub. This friend is a long-time foreign resident of Japan and understood the significance of the neighbouring table's insult. This is what happened.

On his way back from the washroom, he stopped suddenly when he heard some coins fall to the floor. He proceeded to pick them up thinking they were his. A moment later, while seated at our table, he went red in the face.

He'd realized the coins weren't his because his pants pockets didn't have any holes. The coins he'd picked up from the floor were actually thrown at him by the men at the neighbouring table as he'd walked past. The fact that he'd picked up the coins was their way of showing how foreigners always stoop to the lowest level.

"I'm gonna brain ya!" my friend roared.

Luckily for the both of us, he listened to reason and calmed down. I had a momentary flash of jail and deportation.

Staying Calm Despite Others' Hostility

When I was living in Taiwan, I found it particularly irritating that some Taiwanese would always butt in front of me while I was waiting in line to pay for something. The social distance between myself and the customer in front of me was simply seen as opportunity. I wanted to grab that person by the collar, shove him to one side, and give him a lecture in manners—but managed to remember my own upbringing: "Two wrongs don't make a right."

I've also experienced locals getting up and looking for other seats on a train or in a restaurant in Japan when I sat down beside them. It bothered me at first, but these days I'm just grateful for the extra breathing space. At least, I'm not hemmed in like the others.

Back home, of course, I blend in. No one would blink an eye or take notice of me. But here, it's a different story. I stick out like a sore thumb. I don't think it has to do with my height or weight: there are plenty of tall and large-sized Korean, Chinese and Japanese men. It's my skin color, my Caucasian facial features, and my hairiness. I'm a white, hairy male. My looks are different from the norm. They don't stare unabashedly at each other: they know that staring is rude, yet they do it to foreigners. The looks I get range from: "What are you doing here?!" to "Get out of here!" to "Go home! You have no business here!" I usually flash a smile. I'd sometimes like to acknowledge the staring with a quick word or two in their native tongue but I'm not fluent enough. I've often thought that lacking language fluency has a positive aspect in that it shields me from many of the negative comments and insults that are leveled at me without my awareness or direct knowledge.

I live in a small city in central Japan, which is considered rural Japan. I'm surrounded by a ring of mountains with Mt. Asama, an active volcano, visible in the distance. My means of transportation is a bicycle. I cycle everywhere. When I cross paths with local residents, I shout out a "good-morning" or a "hello" in Japanese, but there have been occasions when some Japanese have been startled and shocked by my appearance. They do a double take, then quickly avert their eyes and turn away to avoid looking at me. I see the indignation on their faces and the look of "What is this ugly foreigner doing here?!" and "Get out of my sight!" I tell myself, "Nope I'm not gonna get angry." Getting angry might just land me in hot water.

Visiting Abroad Can Still Be a Positive Experience

Once in Pusan, South Korea, I was waiting for my friends outside a convenience store. A drunk and angry South Korean male came up to me, waving his fist and shouting what I imagined to be verbal abuse in Korean. It could have turned ugly but my friends came out just in the nick of time. We rushed off leaving this wretched man to his rants.

A friend who was teaching there at the time related to another story of mine where some of my young Taiwanese students called me a "pig" in class, and she wanted to know how I reacted. "I just laughed it off and made some oink oink sounds and then got back to the task of teaching," I said. She, however, was deeply hurt and perplexed by the verbal insults shouted by her Korean students.

To tell the truth, I did think that some of the Taiwanese homeroom teachers might do something about this name-calling business, but alas they didn't. They sat there in silence and did nothing. It shocked me since the role of the teacher in Asia is highly esteemed and students are expected to show deference to their teachers.

I've been here long enough now to be over the staring, the scrutinizing, the dirty looks, the fist waving, and the rude behavior. Even though it bothers me at times, I take it in stride. It's part and parcel of the teaching experience in a foreign context. I don't take it to heart. I keep in mind the context and exercise some detachment by maintaining some emotional distance. I don't let it change me.

Because despite these negative encounters, I have had many, many positive experiences. I have met some wonderful people who have become my friends and have taught many students eager to learn English. My understanding of Buddhism has deepened and anyway I immensely enjoy eating Asian foods. . . .

I have the feeling that being involved on a personal and professional level in a host society can lead to positive changes and even break down some of the negative stereotypes that persist. My advice to new expatriates is to focus on your goals and don't get sidetracked by negative experiences or let them interfere with the enjoyment and pleasure of living abroad.

Rutgers's Scarlet Knights Respond to Racism in the Media

C. Vivian Stringer et al.

On the April 4 edition of MSNBC's Imus in the Morning, *talk show personality Don Imus referred to the Rutgers University women's basketball team as "nappy-headed hos." His derogatory comments sparked an immediate response in the media, with many influential people, such as the Reverends Al Sharpton and Jesse Jackson calling for Imus's dismissal from CBS and MSNBC. Although Imus did apologize on the air for his comments, numerous sponsors of the show began to withdraw their support from the program. As a result of the controversy, CBS fired Imus on April 12, 2007.*

On April 10 the Rutgers women's basketball team held a press conference to respond to Imus's comments. The following excerpts from the transcript include responses from head coach C. Vivian Stringer and players Heather Zurich and Essence Carson. The women take pride in their successful efforts on the court during their record-breaking basketball season. They discuss how Imus's comments painfully distracted them from their moment of glory, and they consider the talk-show host's remarks as not only derogatory toward African Americans but also toward all women. The women urge the media to shine their light on the Rutgers women's basketball team not because of this current controversy, but because of the impressive successes the female players have had on the court, in the classroom, and in their personal lives.

C. Vivian Stringer et al., "April 10, 2007 Press Conference Transcribe," www.scarlet knights.com, April 10, 2007. Reproduced by permission.

C. Vivian Stringer: I see 10 young ladies who have accomplished so much that we, the coaching staff, and the State University are proud of. These young ladies who sit before you are valedictorians of their classes, doctors, musical prodigies, and yes, even girl scouts. These young ladies are the best the nation has to offer and we are so very fortunate to have them here at Rutgers. They are ladies of class and distinction; they are articulate, they are brilliant. They are God's representatives in every sense of the word. What you have to realize is less than a year ago half of these ladies were planning to graduate from high school. There are five freshmen who, as they graduated from high school, thought about the opportunity they would have by coming to Rutgers University and by playing basketball at the highest level. Before you know it, everyone here found themselves on a national stage playing for the world to see, playing basketball at the highest level. This group of women is bright, gifted, hard-working and has persevered through so much.

Racist Remarks Hurt

You have all come to talk about this story, this Don Imus story, but we've lost what this is all about. At the beginning of the year we were humiliated as we lost to Duke [University], the number one team in the country. But through perseverance and hard work and dedication, through eight to ten hours working and going through film and studying, ultimately they alone became what they could be when no one else believed in them—that's the greatest story. It doesn't matter where you come from but where you're going. It doesn't matter where you started but how you end because that is the story. Perseverance, hard work, determination. This group of classy young women represents all of us. I have pride and respect for them. What's amazing is less than 24 hours after they accomplished so much to have people insult us. We are all physically, emotionally and mentally spent. We are hurt by the remarks that were uttered by Mr. Imus. But these girls understand that no one can make you feel inferior unless you allow them to. My role as a coach is one to love, nurture and discipline these ladies to leadership roles in this society. In all that we do, this group of young women have been represented as nothing less than class in every aspect of all that they do. While they worked hard in the classroom and accomplished so much and used their gifts and talents, you know, to bring the smiles and the pride within this state in so many people, we had to experience racist and sexist remarks that are deplorable, despicable and abominable and unconscionable. It hurts me.

Imus's Comments Were Sexist, Too

As a sixteen-year old girl, I was a victim of racism but I had a group of people that stood up for me. We (my high school) never had an African American cheerleader and so the chancellor came to my house late one night and asked if I would speak up to the board of education. I initially said no but my dad said some things to me that rang true. He said if you don't stand up for something you'll fall for anything. He said it might not be about you but about future generations of young women. So I went to the school board. I was placed on the cheerleading squad and I became the best I could be. I felt what Mr. Imus said; I've experienced it and I told the team I have experienced it. In my mind, this is a time for change because it's not about just these young women. I ask you, no matter who you are, who could have heard these comments and not been personally offended? It's not about the Rutgers women's basketball team, it's about women. Are women hos? Think about that. Would you want your daughter called a ho? It's not about us as black people or as nappy-headed. It's about us as people—black, white, purple or green. And as much as I speak about that, it's not even black and white—the color is green. How could anyone not have been personally hurt when there is no equality for all or when equality is denied? These young ladies have done nothing wrong. Some of you might point to the fact that he (Don Imus) makes comments about other political figures or other professionals. But these ladies are not professionals or political figures. They are 18, 19, 20 year-old women who came here to get an education and reach their gifts for all to see. These are young women little girls look up to and we as adults, at what point do not call upon people to stop? There is a bigger issue here, more than the basketball team. It's all women athletes, it's all women. Have we lost a sense of our own moral fiber? Has society decayed to such a point where we forgive and forget because it was just a slip of the tongue? I'm going to suggest that people give thought before they speak.

Nuturing Dreams

As a coach, I love them and I cherish them and I appreciate the opportunity to prepare them for the world and prepare them for life. We are preparing them for leadership roles in society. It's never just been a basketball game here for us at Rutgers. It's always been about life. We were so excited, my staff and I, to talk to the recruits because what they saw was a group persevere and beat Duke on Duke's floor. They saw a team that heard people say if you're going to succeed you have to face Michigan in front of 15,000 people. And then they said you have to take on the mighty Duke just to get to the finals. And then face mighty LSU [Louisiana State University] that beat Tennessee a week earlier. Everyone said it wasn't possible with this group of five freshmen and five upperclassmen but this was a group that broke all kinds of NCAA [National Collegiate Athletic Association] records in defense. They showed the world it's not about where you come from but where you're going. It's not about where you start but where you finish. They have restored my confidence and faith as a coach. I respect that their parents would entrust their daughters to me.

Are we as adults responsible enough for nurturing dreams and standing up for what is right? We have to recognize this issue speaks to a bigger issue. To utter such despicable words is not right, whether they are spoken by black, white, purple or green, male or female, tall or short, skinny or thin, it is not right. It is time for everyone to reflect on what is going on. It is time ladies and gentlemen.

I have had the privilege of taking three teams to the Final Four [playoff tournaments]. The first time was with Cheyney [University of Pennsylvania] but I wasn't able to experience it with great joy because my daughter was stricken with meningitis at 14 months and was confined to a wheelchair. With [the University of] Iowa, my husband died suddenly. My heart has never been light when going to the Final Four. When I came to Rutgers we went to the Final Four in 2000 but we never got to the championship game. It took me personally 25 years to come to get to a championship game. This was a team that had so little and gave so much. This was a team that was so young. This was a team that restored all my faith and confidence in young people. They grew and they matured. They all worked together and became a powerful group.

Rutgers University has had a proud reputation for many years as being one of the highest academic institutions in the country. I say to them (the players) and their parents, I thank them for trusting me with their lives and I understand the magnitude of my responsibility and I honor them and am so proud of them. I thank them. They have no reason to drop their heads. I ask everyone who can hear my voice, please understand that we all need to make changes, all of us beyond Imus. We need to serve as examples of how to be winners on the basketball court and we also need to serve as examples of how to be winners in life. I am thankful to serve as coach and I trust that the President of Rutgers, the governor of New Jersey and our Athletic Director to continue their support, respect and honor of these young ladies. I thank you very much. . . .

One Player's Pride

Heather Zurich: Good morning, I am Heather Zurich; A sophomore and a proud member of the Rutgers women's basketball team. This week and last we should have been celebrating our accomplishments this past season; many of the media here, may not realize my team started the season 2–4, we were at the lowest of lows, Coach Stringer called us her worst defensive team ever; but we—the ten of us here—, prevailed, we fought, we persevered and most of all, we believed in ourselves. We won 22 of 25 games to finish the season, before falling to Tennessee in the national championship game. . . . We won the BIG EAST championship along the way, the first ever and advanced to the NCAA Tournament. We know we shocked a lot of people along the way, but this team did not settle for just showing up—we reached what many only dream about—the NCAA title game. But all of our accomplishments were lost. . . . Our moment was taken away, our moment to celebrate our success, our moment to realize how far we came on and off the court as young women; we were stripped of this moment by the degrading comments by Mr. Imus last Wednesday. What hurts the most about this situation is Mr. Imus knows not one of us personally; he doesn't know Mat is the funniest person you will ever meet; Kia is the big sister you never had but always wanted; and Piph would be an unbelievable lawyer someday. These are my teammates, my family. And we were insulted and yes, we are angry. Worst of all, my team and I did nothing to deserve Mr. Imus nor Mr. McGirk's deplorable comments. Our families are upset and with good reason; instead of enjoying our first day off in months to celebrate Easter with our families, this was the topic of conversation. We attend the eighth oldest institution of higher education in the country and not to mention, one of the most difficult academically. (I think many Rutgers students can agree on that.) We ten are simply put—student-athletes. But instead of attending study hall this morning, I address you about something that should never have taken place. I am extremely proud of my teammates—I am proud when we walk through an airport on the way to or from a road trip; dressed alike, in Rutgers gear with pressed pants and nice shoes. The ten of us, love getting dressed up for banquets and I believe we present ourselves well—both on and off the court; even though Mr. Imus seemed to think differently. But then again, he knows not one of us. Thank you for your time. . . .

The Media Should Focus on Rutgers's Glory

Essence Carson: Good morning, my name is Essence Carson and I am a junior student-athlete here at Rutgers University. I would like to express our team's great hurt, anger, and disgust towards the words of Mr. Don Imus. We are highly angered at his remarks but deeply saddened with the racial characterization they entailed. Not only has Mr. Imus stolen a moment of pure grace from us, but he has brought us to the harsh reality that behind the faces of networks that have worked to convey a message of empowerment to young adults, that somehow . . . someway . . . the door has been left open to attack your leaders of tomorrow. You must not forget that we are students first and then athletes . . . and before the student lies the daughter. On collegiate athletics' grandest stage, under the brightest lights, with the focal point being nothing other than a trophy that symbolizes the hard work and perseverance of a team so deserving, the curtains were closed on an act that deserved nothing short of an encore. This Rutgers Women's Basketball team has made history. We were the first team in the school's history to reach a national championship final game. We are a team full of bright-eyed youth that aspire to be great

... not only great on the basketball court, but in the fields of medicine, music, and psychology. I would like to pose a question ... not a question of insult, but one of pure thought.... Where were these major networks when the youth were making history for a prestigious university? Now we are bombarded with cameras, phone calls, and emails that invade our privacy and place us between a rock and a hard place. We haven't done anything to deserve this controversy, but yet it has taken a toll on us mentally and physically. Driven to a point of mental and physical exhaustion, we ask that you not recognize us in a light as dimly lit as this, but in a light that encompasses the great hurdles we've overcome and goals achieved this season. ...

Speaking Out for Equality

I know that rap, hip-hop and music of that genre has desensitized America and this world to some of the words that they choose to use in their lyrics. I understand that, but it doesn't make it any more right for anyone to say it [no]. Not only Mr. Imus, but, if I was to say it, it doesn't make it right. It doesn't make it right if you're African-American, Caucasian, Asian, it doesn't matter. All that matters is that it's wrong. As a society, we're trying to go and trying to surpass that to the point where we don't classify women as hoes. We don't classify African-American women as "nappy-headed hoes". Or anything other than that. Other than the classy women that I believe every woman at this press conference is. ...

I believe there are a lot of positives that can come from this. One thing is that we finally speak up for women, not only African-American women, but all women. That's just going to be a major step forward in society, just to finally understand that keep there isn't that equality that we all wish was there. It's something we all hope for, but until we make those great strides to achieve that, we're going to continue to fall short. I'm glad we're speaking up. I feel like we can achieve that [equality].

CHAPTER 2

Racism at School

Teaching Outside One's Race Can Be a Positive Experience

Bree Picower

Bree Picower is an assistant professor in the Department of Teaching and Learning at New York University's Steinhardt School of Culture, Education, and Human Development. Much of her work explores issues of race and student teachers' ideas about urban education. In the following article Picower reflects on her own experiences as a young white teacher in a mostly African American middle school in Oakland, California. Teaching outside her race proves to be a rewarding experience, as she learns to rethink her role in the classroom, address her own racial identity, and work to address the root causes of racism in order to become a better teacher.

"Oh, the District placed you at Prescott Elementary? You better watch out—they hate white people. Especially that Carrie Secret—she's one of those black radicals, you know, the Ebonics people." This was the warning I was given multiple times in multiple ways when people found out that I had been assigned to Prescott Elementary School for my first reaching position, in Oakland, California in 1999. The "warners" were other white folks who were trying to protect what they saw as a young, new teacher from what they perceived to be a hostile place. However, I really didn't fit the stereotype. I had been involved with several organizations that explicitly addressed issues of race and education for several years, often as the only white person there. I was thrilled to be placed at a school such as Prescott, whose reputation for high achievement for African American children and adoption of the "Ebonics" program had placed it at the forefront of national debate. . . .

Bree Picower, "Teaching Outside One's Race: The Story of an Oakland Teacher," *Radical Teacher*, September 2004, pp. 11–18. Reproduced by permission.

Prescott Elementary School

When I was first assigned to Prescott, I drove to the school to see what it was like. It was summer and the school was gated and locked. From the outside, it looked like a barren and dismal place. There was no grass, no playground. only a huge, concrete excuse for a yard. The main building and the portables were all a drab shade of industrial yellow. When I was finally able to enter the school weeks later, the difference between what I had seen from outside the gate, and the reality of what it was really like inside was like night and day. The walls inside the main building were covered with a vibrant mural tracing leaders of African American history. Even before the school year started, kids were everywhere, helping teachers set up their rooms, playing in the yard, and welcoming me and the other new teachers. The children, primarily African American, but also Latino and Asian American, seemed to feel so at home at the school, as if they had a real sense of ownership of the place. Because I wasn't initially assigned to a room or grade, I took the opportunity to walk around and introduce myself and help the other teachers. When I did finally get my own room, filthy from being used as a storage space by construction workers, many children, from kindergartners to graduated middle schoolers, came by to help me unpack.

My class was a second and third grade Sheltered English class which consisted of a very diverse group of students reflecting the multilingual community of Oakland. While Prescott as a whole was primarily African American, my students were Guatemalan, El Salvadorian, Cambodian, Filipino, and Arabic as well as African American children. My classroom was in a building off the main school that housed three classrooms—mine, Carrie Secret's, and that of another teacher whom I had also been warned about—Aileen Moffitt. I had been told that I should align myself with Ms. Moffitt because she was "the only white person that has ever been accepted at Prescott."

Afrocentric Environment and Culturally Relevant Teaching

The political nature of the school soon became obvious. Walking into the classrooms and viewing the bulletin boards of the veteran teachers, I could easily see how central African American history was to the school. The library was filled with multicultural texts. Carrie's and Aileen's rooms were explosions of color, with paintings, posters, and photographs dedicated to telling the story of African American people. The school assembly calendar, handed out the first day of school, listed events honoring not only Black history, but Mexican history, Cambodian dance, and multicultural art.

I breathed deep and knew I had found my home. It seemed that the teachers here fit [philosopher, scholar, and author] Gloria Ladson-Billings's definition of culturally relevant teachers [in *Crossing Over to Canaan: The Journey of New Teachers in Diverse Classrooms*]. "They see themselves as a part of the community and they see teaching as giving back to the community. They help students make connections between their local, national, racial, cultural, and global identities." This was the kind of teaching that I longed to do, and I was relieved that I had found a place where it was not only going to he safe to do it, but it would also be valued and accepted. I couldn't believe my luck.

Veteran teachers who came by my room saw the same kind of respect for cultural diversity reflected on my walls, and it wasn't long before they were sharing materials and ideas to help me with my teaching practice. After Miss Moffitt saw me at the copy machine reproducing U.S. maps depicting European colonization and diminishing Native American land, she came by my room to give me a song about Columbus. The lyrics began:

> In fourteen-hundred-ninety-two, Columbus sailed the ocean blue. It was a courageous thing to do, But someone was already there.

The song goes on to describe the destruction of the land of various Native American tribes, the ensuing slavery, and the spread of disease that decimated the people. My class performed this at the Thanksgiving assembly along with other students who celebrated Native American dance and recited poetry about different forms of colonialism. Because my personal philosophy was so closely aligned with the mission of the school, this year was turning out to be a powerful and positive experience for me. . . .

Ebonics and the Standard English Program (SEP)

What did the Ebonics controversy have to do with Prescott? Right before the school year started, I lay tossing and turning at three in the morning, worried about my first teaching experience. I suddenly remembered a back issue of *Rethinking Schools* that had addressed the national debate around the controversy. I stumbled to my file cabinet and pulled it out, opening to an interview with, that's right, Carrie Secret. The interview . . . chronicles the controversy that erupted in Oakland in 1996. It described the high academic performance at Prescott Elementary as an anomaly in the District. . . .

It was Prescott's success with teaching African American children that motivated the district to adopt SEP [Standard English Proficiency], igniting the flames of the media across the country. A great deal of research has been done to document the way in which the media misrepresented the District's decision to use SEP to improve the achievement gap. J.R. Rickford and R.J. Rickford carefully analyze the events around the school board's adoption of SEP and the media's reaction to it [in *Spoken Soul: The Story of Black English*]. "The Oakland school board never intended to replace the teaching of Standard or mainstream English with the teaching of Ebonics, or Spoken Soul. But it did intend to take the vernacular into account in helping students achieve mastery of Standard English (reading and writing in this variety in particular)". In *Rethinking School*, Carrie Secret explained, "There's a misconception of the program, created by the media blitz of misinformation. Our mission was and continues to be: embrace and respect Ebonics, the home language of many of our students, and use strategies that will move them to a competency level in English. We never had, nor do we now have, any intention of teaching the home language to students. They come to us speaking the language.". . .

At no point in my training or time at Prescott was I taught to or expected to speak or teach Ebonics to my students, just as I was not expected to teach Khmer, Spanish, or Arabic. Rather, teachers were encouraged to teach in ways that celebrated and reflected our students' cultures. Ebonics was spoken throughout the school because Prescott promoted the home culture of the student and teachers were expected to understand Ebonics because it was the home language of the majority of the students. It was our responsibility to help the students translate their home language into Standard English. The way this was done was the same way I was trained to do with all of my second language learners, through techniques designed to familiarize and contrast their language with Standard English. . . .

Racial Identity and Politics at Prescott

Because of the nature of our staff development, racial identity, racism, Afrocentricity, and white supremacy were central topics of conversation at Prescott. The staff at the school was both racially and generationally mixed. Becoming a part of the leadership structure of the school, or gaining insider status, appeared at first glance to be dependent on race. However, it became apparent as time went on that it had more to do with your level of commitment to the mission of the school, which in turn had much to do with where individuals were in the development of their racial identity. . . .

Because of the diversity of the Prescott staff, who they were and where they came from directly influenced their racial identity development, and therefore their status at the school. . . .

I believe a major period of development for me was in the early nineties when I was employed at a community center that worked to meet the needs of the residents of three public housing sites in Ann Arbor, Michigan. The center was directed by Rose Martin, an African American woman who grew up in over 12 foster families and had overcome her own struggles with drugs and alcohol. The center was staffed with people who had all been born and raised in the community. Starting as a volunteer, and eventually being offered a job, I was one of the only two white people who worked there. Having grown up in New York City, I was accustomed to and comfortable in diverse settings, but this was the first time that I was the real minority. I worked there for four years, eventually co-directing all K-6 programming. During my stay, I learned a great deal about that particular community and, more generally, how to live with, work with, respect, and be respected by people of color. I had to reflect upon my own identity as a white person, because much of my way of thinking, being, and acting was different from that of the people I spent every day with. I gained an appreciation for the importance of leadership of color when working with communities of color, having worked in prior settings that were "serving" black children, but that were run by white adults. Working as a liaison between my students' families and their teachers, I was confronted directly with the ways in which the Ann Arbor schools were not meeting their needs, often arising out of a cultural mismatch between students and teachers.

After several years and a move to California, I began working at the Bay Area Coalition of Essential Schools, working with schools to close the achievement gap between black and white students while raising overall achievement. Through this work, I was explicitly addressing issues of equity and race with racially diverse faculties. . . . These two experiences gave me the opportunity to identify and reflect upon my whiteness, to recognize types of white supremacy and racism. . . .

Because of this background, I was developmentally "ready" to be a member of the Prescott community, participating in an environment with an African American leadership structure and an explicit focus on race and racism. . . .

Conflicts Between White and Black

Many new white teachers see whiteness as the absence of race, or only recognize it in opposition to "others" and this leads to a level of discomfort when issues of race are raised. Having lived in and among primarily other whites, many whites see themselves as part of a "racial norm" and believe that they are "color blind," holding no prejudices towards others. This "color blindness" stops them from seeing who the students really are and the cultures that they bring with them to the classroom, and therefore limits the educational strategies that they can draw upon to teach them. At a school like Prescott, not being able to recognize culture caused whites at this stage of development to feel alienated by the racially charged discussions that permeated the school. Many of them came to teaching because they "loved children" and did not understand why "we always have to talk about race." Many of these teachers believed that they had not been accepted by the staff of Prescott, and felt uncomfortable at the school. . . .

I found that for myself, and several other newer teachers, entering the school with a desire to learn from the veteran African American teachers about the Standard English Program and culturally competent teaching pedagogy was one way to earn acceptance. The veteran teachers, the "insiders" who had been there for twenty to thirty years, had seen the full range of white attitudes that had come to the school, from the missionary to the hippie, all thinking that they knew what it

51

would take to "save these poor kids." This attitude, reinforced and reflected in popular movies such as *Dangerous Minds* and *Music from the Heart*, showed white teachers who seemed to have all the answers and were able to rescue black and brown students from their misguided communities.

In reality at Prescott, every day was a struggle for these white teachers. It was striking to see the difference between the way students in the veteran African-American teachers' classrooms behaved and the way the students in the new, white teachers' rooms behaved. Something about the structure and relationships between the new teachers and their students reinforced the worst stereotypes of both groups. The students ran around, rarely listened, and talked back. The teachers yelled, threatened, cried, and complained. The black teachers yelled often as well, but there was something different in the tone of the yelling. It was more of a mother's voice pushing their child, not a yell coming from a place of lack of control or of fear. Their students were no angels, but their rooms were structured, the environments were warm, and learning was obviously taking place.

This exact issue of the racial difference in the tone of yelling was brought to the table at a staff meeting my second year at Prescott. It came up during a discussion in which several new teachers claimed that they felt no support at Prescott from the veteran teachers. The veteran teachers answered that the young teachers had no interest in learning from them and had never attempted to seek support. They were angry that the new teachers were clearly failing and were apparently doing nothing to try to improve their practice. The veteran teachers couldn't understand; why hadn't they knocked on the door of the older teachers and asked for help? Leslie Morrison, a newer black teacher, and I raised the issue that we had felt very supported, but that at Prescott, you have to prove to the veteran staff what your intentions are and that you are willing to learn from them. Because of their stage of racial identity development, many white teachers were unwilling to recognize culture as an issue, or as a doorway for success with their students. Therefore they did not benefit from the staff development at the school, and did not know how to participate in the community.

I remember early on a debate that erupted during a meeting in which grade level teachers were charting what skills and knowledge they wanted their students to enter their classroom with at the beginning of the year. The charts were then to be shared with the teachers of the prior grade so that they could be used as a scope and sequence for the year. Ms. Charles, a veteran African American teacher with an outstanding record of success with her students, was telling Ms. Kelly, a second year, white kindergarten teacher, what she expected her students to be able to do in math when starting first grade. She was outraged by how low in skills her new class was and blamed the current kindergarten teachers and their low expectations. The low expectations were clearly identifiable by what was written on the kindergarten chart. (The kindergarten teachers had charted what they planned on teaching that year—since they couldn't control what level of education the students came to school with.) When this chart was shown to the whole staff, Carrie, Ms. Drew, and other veteran teachers exploded. Carrie confronted the newer teachers and declared that she remembered when the kids came with higher skills because the black kindergarten teachers that used to be there believed in their students and pushed them to higher levels. . . .

Lessons Learned

My real teacher education did not happen in a pre-service program, but rather came from educators of color, such as Rose Martin and Carrie Secret, who taught me about the importance of relationships and culture in reaching children. Being successful in an environment such as Prescott is not something that a "methods" course could ever teach in a semester.

It requires a commitment to the cause of social justice and a true desire to change the inequities that exist within the current structure of education. It requires expanding the idea of a classroom from being a room with four walls to the community it is situated in, where you are both the teacher and the learner at the same time. It requires building real relationships with the people you are working with or for and seeing your students and their families as your employer rather than your administrators and superintendents. It requires explicitly addressing your own racial identity and taking responsibility for how it informs your interactions and power dynamics with others. Finally, it requires a continual quest for both learning more and doing more to address the root causes of racism and white supremacy in order to really teach the children you are hoping to educate.

I Was a Victim of Racial Violence in Junior High

Anonymous, as written to Cary Tennis

An anonymous adult white woman writes to Cary Tennis, writer of the "Since You Asked" column at Salon *magazine, to explain how she was physically and emotionally abused by black children in junior high. Today she feels like a racist for still being afraid of black people.*

When I was starting junior high, my family moved to a medium-sized city in the Midwest. My parents bought a house in the best school district in the city and sent me and my brother to the public school around the corner.

At my public school, there was something called voluntary desegregation, which entailed packing poor (black) kids from the decaying inner city onto buses and sending them to the rich (white) school districts so they could get a better education than what was offered in the inner-city schools. The program was well intentioned and, with better implementation, could have been excellent. However, the administration hadn't thought to give teachers extra resources or training to help these kids, who faced some different challenges than the teachers were used to, nor did they think to give teachers, parents or kids any sensitivity training. Therefore, the cultural climate at the school was at best tense and at worst a disaster. There were black tables and white tables in the lunchroom, black and white hallways, black and white corners of the gym. The black kids and the white kids sat separately in the classrooms. All of this was student imposed and unspoken. This was my first experience with diversity.

The abuse started about halfway through sixth grade. I had not been able to make friends with any of my black classmates—I was friendly, albeit somewhat socially awkward, but my overtures were rejected—and one day, a black girl decided she hated me, as 13-year-old girls are wont to do. She and her friends, both male and female, began to beat me up, kick me, punch me, rip up my homework and deny it all to the teacher. I was once thrown down a flight of stairs and narrowly escaped breaking my neck. I appealed to the school, as did my parents, but the administration refused to punish the perpetrators, claiming that it would be taken as racism. I, however, would be punished for defending myself in any way. The administration followed through on this; my parents enrolled me in self-defense classes, and when I blocked a punch at one point, I was given an in-school suspension. My abusers were never punished.

To this day, I don't know why I in particular was targeted; who knows why kids target one another? In any case, this went on for two years, until the ringleader of the girls left the school—I never found out why—and the others slowly stopped beating me up, preferring to ignore me. By the time high school rolled around, I was no longer abused, except for the occasional "f--- cracker" comment, but the racial climate was such that the black kids and the white kids almost never spoke to or socialized with one another. Even the classes were mostly segregated, with my honors and advanced-placement classes being almost exclusively white and the remedial classes being almost exclusively black.

Part of Me Remains Scared

Looking back now, as a grad student in my early 20s, I can understand, to a certain extent, the sources of these tensions. I've studied my American history and read my [Frantz] Fanon [an author and prominent contributor to postcolonial studies], and I feel mostly compassion for my long-ago attackers.

But I am furious at my old school district, not only for denying me the protection I needed but for allowing a more insidious sort of segregation to persist inside its walls and for denying many of the kids from the inner city the educational support they were due. But when you're 13 and vulnerable, and you can't figure out why people hate you so much that they want to hurt you, and nothing you can do will get them to stop, and no one will help you, you don't think in terms of civil rights and class divisions and historic injustices. You just see a group of people who hate you for no reason that you can fathom, and you're terrified of them.

And that's the problem. Part of me remains that scared 13-year-old. To this day, when I see a group of young black people standing together in a group, my heart starts to race and I have to force myself not to avoid them. If I'm standing on a train platform with a group of black youths, I am irrationally scared that they're going to push me in front of a train. My earliest experience with black people was incredibly traumatic, and I'm still feeling the aftershocks from that trauma. The fear has faded somewhat over the years, but every so often it flares back into life, and it makes me sick and angry with myself and ashamed.

I hate feeling like a racist, because racism goes against my deepest-held beliefs and values. I truly believe that race is a constructed concept and that all men and women are created equal, and my group of close friends is now very diverse and includes a lovely black woman. I'm getting an M.A. [master of arts] in post-colonial literature and theory. Intellectually and in practice, I am as far from being racist as one can get. But my fight-or-flight response is stubborn in its memory and it reacts to dark skin like a phobia.

Do I Feel Included at MIT?
Not Really

Pius A. Uzamere II

As a sophomore electrical engineering and computer science major at Massachusetts Institute of Technology (MIT), Pius A. Uzamere II of Newcastle, Pennsylvania, won the third annual Dr. Martin Luther King Jr. Oratory Contest. In his award speech Uzamere says that despite the fact that he is a proud African American, he does not feel completely included in American society. He points out the racial inequalities he has experienced in his life, and he urges his peers at MIT to stop the practice of self-segregation by racial groups on campus.

My name is Pius Afrikase Uyiosa Uzamere II. I am a proud African-American male. My father is Nigerian and black, while my mother is American and white. I can vote. I attend the best school in the world. My roommate is white and my friends span all different races. I use the same water fountains as anyone else. No one in my family has ever undergone the tragedy of involuntary servitude. No one has ever called me nigger to my face. I suspect that few people at MIT [Massachusetts Institute of Technology] have the audacity to ever say such a thing to me in person.

So I'm a black male and I have many opportunities. Right now, in the year 2002, almost four decades after the death of the Rev. Martin Luther King Jr., are blacks in this country considered a mainstream part of society? Is my race fully included here?

I think that most people outside of my race feel that the answer to this question is yes. So many people pay lip service

Pius A. Uzamere II, "EECS Sophomore Wins Martin Luther King Oratory Contest," web.mit.edu, March 20, 2002. Reproduced by permission. This article originally appeared on the MIT News Office Web Site.

to the equal treatment of all races that it must be true. As a matter of fact, during my senior year of high school, I spent two hours trying to convince one of my white teachers that racism still exists in this country.

Despite what others may think, I believe that the answer is no. Full inclusion of black people in America is an illusion. You don't believe me? Perhaps I should reintroduce myself.

Inclusion Is an Illusion

My name is Pius. I asked a girl from a different race out once and she told me that it wouldn't work because I was black. In the last presidential election, people of my race were systematically turned away from the polls in Florida. I've had only one black teacher in my entire life, including here [at MIT]. In high school, I was the only black person in my honors classes even though my school had 400 black students. I'm a black male. On any given day, nearly one in eight of us aged 20 to 34 are in jail or prison. I've walked into stores with a suit on and still had nervous clerks eyeing me suspiciously, following me from behind, and wondering whether I'm going to steal the trinkets they want to sell me. Last year, I was walking down Amherst Alley on a cold day and a white fraternity member, a person whom I had never met, threw water balloons at me from a window and shouted, "I hate you. I f—ing hate you!"

So do I feel included? Not really. We've come a long way, to be sure. Dr. King's efforts have pushed us incredibly far, especially with respect to legislative remedies for the problem. However, I fear that the social taboo that now prevents most racists from espousing their hateful beliefs leads to a dangerous condition—one where the racism is subtle and taken for granted. No, in today's world, racism usually isn't apparent from what people say to your face. Rather it's what they say behind your back, it's how they act with their friends in private, it's the things they do without thinking. Often, the prejudices I see are so well-ingrained in the characters of the people I talk to, that they say something patently offensive and obviously have no idea that they said anything wrong. The problem of eliminating the racist preconceptions that many have is a hard problem, much harder than the problem of eliminating racist laws.

Self-Segregating Campus

I wish I had the full solution to the problem. But I don't. Briefly though, I'll try my hand at a piece of the solution. Here at MIT, I think that a great barrier that needs to be overcome is the problem of self-segregation. A friend of mine made the comment that "voluntary segregation (on this campus) is much more about selecting who you are not friends with rather than who you are friends with."

That's really important. Sure, it's not a sin to have friends of only a certain race. Unfortunately, most of these self-segregated groups are also exclusive when it comes to choosing friends. Furthermore, in most cases, it's indicative of more deeply rooted issues. As I said, I think most people here would find it pretty unacceptable for someone to call me a nigger in public. However, I suspect that many of the people who would decry such a blatant display of racism would also be the same people who won't talk to me when they are with friends of their own race. Some of these same people find the thought of dating someone of my race absolutely unthinkable. Many of these same people, whether they say it or not, are surprised to find that I'm black and I don't speak ebonics. These are the same people who look at the ceiling and pretend they don't see me when I pass them in the Infinite Corridor, even though I live down the hall.

This is a big problem that cuts across most minority groups here at MIT. Black, Chinese, Puerto Rican, Indian, you name it. Interestingly enough, I've found that, in general, the race least guilty of this on campus is the "majority"—white people. The minorities tend to be the most exclusive in my experience. For an example, within my own race, I've witnessed black cliques enter a room of people they don't know and be rather unfriendly to white people who approach them. Not overtly rude, of course, but they make very little effort to make these people feel welcome. Yet, the first new black person to approach them is quickly befriended by the group.

This self-segregating behavior hurts much more than it helps. Fine, self-segregation allows you to stay within your comfort zone. Big deal. Meanwhile, you serve to alienate others and perpetuate any negative stereotypes they may have of people in your group. The main root of most of the ignorant prejudices people have is a lack of communication. It's hard to maintain ignorant preconceptions of people after you actually talk to them regularly. I think that if we can overcome this issue in our community, we'll go a long way to improving the inclusion we feel in our daily lives.

Racism Exists
in Graduate School

Rose Rodriguez-Rabin

Rose Rodriguez-Rabin is a lecturer in the Freshman Initiative Writing Program at the University of Texas at San Antonio. She was surprised to encounter racism because of her Native American heritage when she left her home in the South to attend graduate school in the Midwest. In graduate school, she recalls that her peers expressed no interest in her cultural background, yet they assumed that she would secure later employment through affirmative action initiatives, because of her race and not her academic talents. Although her experiences with racism in college cause her to lose a sense of her self, she is later able to regain her identity and share her experiences with her own students.

I left my life back south. Everyone, friends and family, was excited for me. No one could believe I was actually going to graduate school—the first in my family. I felt like I was floating on a cloud. My father always wanted me to go to college; my mother just wanted me to marry well. My colleagues patted me on the back. "We knew you would amount to something." My husband just stared off into empty space. "Are you sure this is what you want?"

All my life, my skin color meant nothing to me. It is just a part of who I am, nothing more, nothing less. I know I am stubborn. I do not give up easily. I know I love to read, I love to write, and nothing is more important to me than learning. All I ever wanted to do was learn. My graduate school experience in the Midwest was just that, a learning experience. I learned I was the wrong color. I learned silence is best in a predominately white institution. I learned that in the Midwest, my voice was the voice of my color, especially when I was the only person of "color" in the classroom. I learned how much I could take and also how much I could not take. I learned I should not have left the south. I learned I should have listened to my now ex-husband. I learned how to be silent. I learned I was caught between two worlds: my people and my ambitions.

Going to College Can Change You

All I ever wanted to do was learn. Leaving my hometown, I expected to gather all the information and knowledge I could muster and take it back home. Home. Home, where the people are the same color as me. Home, where people accept me for who I am, or now, who I was. In reality, once a person of color leaves his/her hometown, they cannot go back. Your family looks at you differently, and they treat you differently. I cannot even change the oil in my truck without being told to go sit down and do what I normally do: read. With awkward looks and mixed emotions, I go to the truck seat that sits on the oil stained concrete and try to read.

My first stories came from the mechanics garage that was my second home. My lessons about reality and fantasy came from here, and now I am being told by my surrogate father to take a seat. He would change the oil in my truck, when previously I was told I had two capable hands and I could change my own oil. Funny what going to school does to you, and for you.

All I ever wanted to do was learn. My experiences at school have been no different. Like I mentioned earlier, I did not know my skin color until I started attending graduate school; fake smiles, fake endearments, and two-faced realities. What was I doing here? I just wanted to learn. People at first treated me with respect, but once I spoke, it was as if I turned my back on them. Me, submissive? No. Me, tolerant of racist remarks? Never. Once I was accused of throwing my "Indianness" at my classmates. Why? Because my skin color is not white? Why? Because I proudly chose to wear my Indian choker to class? Or is it because they have no culture to proudly display? I do not know and still do not understand.

Racist Comments Should Not Go Unchallenged

I was the only person of color in a particular graduate class, but at first I did not feel any different. I was just a student who wanted to learn. But there was another particular student who was allowed to make racist and egotistical remarks. Never once did the professor reprimand that student. I am not sure if the student was reprimanded outside of class, but I do know that he kept on with the remarks throughout the semester. I stared into every face to see if they reacted or understood what he said. Emotionless, blank faces. Was I the only one who was catching these remarks? "Oh, you are just being super sensitive," I was told. Was I? Again, a remark was made. It was overlooked. Again, and again. Blank faces. Was I being super sensitive? Am I just misunderstanding? What was wrong with me?

The day came when enough was enough. My comments were always questioned and even challenged in this class, but nothing was ever brought up about the other student's comments. Enough was enough. I walked out of class. I thought that would bring to light the situation at hand. Next was a meeting with the professor and others. I explained my frustrations, I explained my actions. Pale, blank faces looked back at me. Emotionless. "We have this dream for you," I was told. Dream? For me? "You can help us teach this class," I was told. How? Examples that people "like me" have a brain? We can think for ourselves? That possibly we have our own dreams? Yes, I have dreams, too, and they did not include that class and that professor or any of the administration in that department. "I have my own dreams," I screamed in my head with frustration. At that moment, tears ran down my hot cheeks. Fruitless. Pale, blank faces looked back at me.

My History Was Not Valued by My Peers

All I wanted to do was learn. But all I got was cynicism, all I felt was regret. I realized now that I did not fit in with my own people, and I did not fit into this institution. "Nonwhite" faces searching for other "nonwhite" faces. My ideas were questioned. Shakespeare, Chaucer, Milton—those are not the writers of my people. Chuy, Dago, Norma, Paula, and Sandra are the writers of my people, but because my people express themselves through oral narratives, my history does not count. The stories I chose to read are not valuable or viable in a predominately white institution. "Chaucer and Milton are the classics," I was told. My response, "So is Paula, Norma, and others. They are the classics." My classmates retorted, "As considered by whom?" My response, "As considered by my teachings." Then I was considered unteachable and labeled by my so-called peers as a super sensitive troublemaker. "Join a Native Lit. class," I was told. "No, you need to get into a Native Lit. class. Maybe you will learn something," I retorted. Silence.

All I wanted to do was learn. Because of my situation at school, I wrote religiously. I wrote. I joined a writers group in school. Finally, I can share my work with some of my classmates. My work was basic writing, my research topic on the South. "Please leave a copy of your paper in each member's box. The meeting will take place here and at this time." "Great! Finally an outlet," I thought to myself. The day came. I grabbed my paper, I grabbed my coat, and excited about the possibility of getting feedback on my writing, I hurried to school. I walked into the classroom. "Hmm. I can't believe I am the first one here," I thought to myself. "I must really be eager. How embarrassing." I took off my coat, placed it behind my seat, put my folder on the desk, and took out my paper. I sat on the desk and waited. Ten minutes after, and I waited. Fifteen minutes later; I wiggled in my seat. I began to read my paper. I wondered what kind of suggestions I was going to get on my paper. Twenty minutes later. "Okay, where in the hell is everyone?" I thought to myself. Thirty-five minutes later, no one showed up. Tears began to well up in my eyes. Defeat.

Frustration. It was forty-some minutes since the meeting was supposed to have begun, and no one showed up. I grabbed my coat and walked to look in my mailbox in the office to see if there was a message. Nothing. Fine. Tears again. I put on my coat and hugged my folder. I walked out of the building with welled-up eyes. Fine.

The next day, I got little notes with written excuses. "Sorry I couldn't make it . . ." "Hey, I read your piece. Pretty cool." "Sorry I couldn't show up," and so on. It did not matter to me anymore. They made their point. After that day, I never again received a notice of upcoming meetings, nor did I care— anymore.

I Am Not a Match to Others

All I wanted to do was learn. Okay, I was going to have to face the reality that I was not going to get the intellectual stimulation I so desperately needed from school. Where could I get it? Conferences. Kansas City. Little did I know that is where the Indian people look at you and determine if you are Indian or not. "Who is your family? Where are you from? You carry a card? What rez does your family live on? You look Indian? Are you?" "Naw man, I just had plastic surgery," I thought to myself. The panels were all these Native men telling me how to be a real Indian. I felt like I was in a Sherman Alexie [Native American author and screenwriter] movie. To be Indian you need to. . . . The worst incident was with a professor from Kansas who is the authority on Indianness. "Where are you from?" he asked me. Followed by, "Who are your people?"

And then, "There are no Indians in . . ." I looked at him dead in the eyes. "How do you know?" I asked. "Have you been reading white man's history books?" I asked. My retort to professor so and so was, "My people refused to be locked up on a rez like animals, and refused to carry a card like some concentration camp prisoner, but instead chose to flee south where they could do as they pleased and not acculturate as they saw fit, like some people I know." Cold, pale, blank stares. I turned on my heels and left Kansas City, left the so-called Indian conference and returned to a white man's institution.

All I wanted to do was learn. I sat at my desk in an office I shared with three other "peers," officemates as we are called. We are put together to help each other out, to support one another in times of need. Again, I am the only nonwhite person in the area. The office is decorated with fancy little plastic flowers, cute, matching desk sets are placed on top of the desks. Filing cabinets are identified with labels as to whose is whose. In my area of the office is a poster of all the Native American tribes in America, a nice "real" green plant, a desk calendar from the Air Force that I snagged from the local school gathering, a picture of Benicio del Toro taped to my side of the filing cabinet. That was my desk. Nothing matched and it did not matter.

Intelligence Should Bring Rewards, Not Skin Color

One of my officemates comes in distressed about the possibility of finding a job after graduation. We try to reassure her she will not have any problems. But she looks at me and coldly says, "You won't have a problem finding a job because of who you are." Shock. "What is that supposed to mean?" I asked myself. Second thinking sets in.

I call a meeting with my committee. I tell them not to lie to me and give it to me straight. "Will I be able to find a job after I graduate?" They, without hesitation, respond yes, I will.

"Why, because of my color?" I asked. "No, you have a unique dissertation topic . . ." Relief. A sigh of relief. We talk about my possibilities. I leave the meeting feeling good about myself and my work. Again, back in the office, one of my officemates asks how my meeting with the committee went, and I say it went well. I know I will get a job after graduation, and not because of my skin color, as was insinuated earlier, but because of my dissertation topic. Shock sets in in the office. Silence. "You don't have to be vengeful," I was told. I was not being vengeful. "They just told you that because they are your committee." "No, I was told that because they have faith in me and they know I have a brain. I think for myself and don't follow anyone else's lead. I am me, and I am my own person. Thank you for having faith in me," was my response.

All I wanted to do was learn. I sure learned a lot. I learned I did not fit in with my family anymore; I learned I did not fit in the ivory tower; and then I learned I did not fit in the Indian community because I did not carry a card, nor was I born and raised on a reservation. So where do I fit in? Nowhere. Breakdown and leave. The few people I met in that ivory tower are the few people that have helped keep me sane. The few people I still talk to from the ivory tower are the people I still hold close to my heart. Other than that, that ivory tower can crumble, and crumble it is. No more Native students.

Racism Does Not Have to Weaken Your Sense of Self

I left my life in the Midwest and headed south for winter, as my people used to do when they followed the buffalo. I did not want to read anymore, I could not write, and I never wanted to learn again. My soul was stolen. It lies somewhere buried in the Midwest snow.

It has taken me almost two years to regain my identity. It has taken me two years to write, to want to read, and to want to learn. I am not defeated. I am teaching now. I have my life again in the south. Same state, different city. My new home. I am teaching now and working on my program again. I will not be defeated.

First day of classes; I announce who I am and what I am doing here. I explain how I got here and where I plan on going. I will not be stopped this time. I have regrouped, grounded myself, and my self-identity is stronger now.

Second day of classes; my students want to know about my tribe. I explain some, tell them to read about the rest. They want to know about my life in graduate school. I am shocked at first, but I then go on to explain that it was a learning experience. They ask for more details. I tell them about my friends I miss, I tell them about the few professors I admire, and how one actually wrote me two years later and apologized for not reprimanding the other students for their racist remarks.

Third day of classes; we read Sherman Alexie's [short story] "Indian Education." The students, who are of all nationalities and races and cultures, respond well. The discussion is good. A lot of positive feedback.

But later that evening, I get a call from the composition coordinator. "We have a problem." Silence. "One of your students has filed a complaint against you." The coordinator assures me that they will stand behind me and support whatever move I decide to make. "You are an asset to this school and we don't want to lose you. We have moved her from your class." Silence. "She wrote, 'I feel I am being oppressed because I am white,'" he said. Laughter. "Can you imagine that? She's being oppressed? You just happen to find the only student in this state who is from the Midwest." Laughter on both ends. "I am sorry she has left your class. Obviously she wasn't interested in learning." Silence.

All I ever wanted to do was learn.

CHAPTER 3

Racism, Tragedy, and Violence

Post 9/11 America Is a Tough Place for South Asians

Janes Gregoire and Myles Miller

Janes Gregoire and Myles Miller from Children's PressLine, a journalism program for young people ages eight to eighteen in New York City, discussed the topic of life in America after 9/11 with three young organizers from the group, Desis Rising Up and Moving (DRUM). A Desi is anyone of South Asian ancestry, and DRUM is a nonprofit organization devoted to educating others about the ways that Americans' reactions to 9/11 have changed Desi communities. The three DRUM members discuss the difficulty of preventing racism in light of the American media's response to 9/11. They reflect on the backlash of racism that Desis have encountered because of the terrorist attacks. And they consider the effects of racial profiling and other national policies that have emerged since the 9/11 tragedy.

Raheed, 17: Racism Is Hard to Prevent

I was born and raised in Saudi Arabia and my parents are from Bangladesh. I have been in the United States for two years. 9/11 was scary, from the fact that I was coming from Saudi Arabia. When I saw it on TV, for a few seconds I thought, "Oh, they're making a new movie or something." But then when it said "Live," I got so scared . . . it was like war was about to happen or something.

After 9/11 there has been a lot of racism. When I went to school, people didn't know where I came from. I had a friend who later on when he found out that I came from Saudi Arabia, said a lot of stuff like, "Oh, what so [terrorist] Osama [bin Laden] is your uncle or something?" and, "In Saudi Arabia, do they teach you to shoot AK47s in school?" It's really

Janes Gregoire and Myles Miller, "Post 9/11 America Is A Tough Place for Young Desis," *Children's PressLine*, October 13, 2006. Reproduced by permission.

messed up. I was kind of racist before, but then after that I realized how hurtful it might be and then I wished I could do something about it. It made me realize how messed up the society can get sometimes.

Nowadays, if the youth hear something messed up they'll just go punch somebody, knock somebody out. But to prevent [racism], talk it out. I don't know how much it works; I was never in a situation where I tried to prevent it. Like my friend, I didn't try to stop him saying it, it's just that I'm not friends with him anymore.

Shoshi, 20:
9/11 Caused a Backlash of Racism

I am originally from Bangladesh. On 9/11 I was in New York City in my high school. After that I really saw the panic in the Muslim community, how that affected them, and all of the backlashes and hate crimes that were done against them.

Right after 9/11, we really started seeing the fear in our community, especially South Asian, Arab, Muslim communities where people were afraid to go out of the house or even do anything. At that time in DRUM [Desis Rising Up and Moving] we started doing an outreach flyer. We used to go to different neighborhoods where there was a high population of South Asian folks and put these flyers up that basically stated: If you have been the victim of a hate crime or if you have been abused or raided by FBI agents, you need to call us and that's our hotline. So at that time we were getting a lot of calls about people saying that they were getting raided in their house or their brothers or fathers were getting taken away from them by the FBI coming into their homes.

In 2001, the Patriot Act was passed and also the Special Registration Program was done in New York City that required men or boys 16 and over to go register from 25 different countries and every one was a Muslim country except for North Korea. A lot of the calls that came in were very emotional and very saddening. Brothers and fathers that were just taken away from their homes, or they went to register thinking that they were complying with the government and they ended up being in detention centers and later being deported. Really, at that time, we were seeing how government agencies like the FBI or the police department were going into our homes and breaking up our families and tearing them apart.

The Media Increases Racism

Throughout history, the backlashes and the hatred that our community and people of color in general have faced when they enter this country shows that we don't have equal access to anything, especially if you are undocumented. You don't have access to healthcare, you don't have access to school or higher education. Just seeing that has heavily influenced me in doing this political work that I'm doing now.

Right after 9/11, the media played a big role in portraying Muslims as being terrorists or Muslims being bad and a lot of the hate crimes increased. We're seeing that it's not just that one day you wake up and decide to hate all of the Muslims. It's that something is put into your mind that does that. The media has a big role in doing that. So actually exposing the media or the government in how they're being racist and treating our folks differently.

Just understanding what's going on, like our anger and our frustration, there are healthy ways to portray those and actually push for social change. It's a really great feeling to know that you're actually making positive changes in your community. Change is possible; we haven't hit the dead end. There's no such thing as "that's just the way it is."

Rashi, 20:
Policing a Problem Does Not Solve It

Political education is really crucial because sometimes many of the things you see on TV or read in the newspaper is just one point of view. It's not really coming from the communities themselves; it's basically just corporate or government agencies that are putting out these messages. You're not really hearing the side of the people from the communities.

After 9/11, all of the hate crimes that were happening made me realize that sometimes people don't get all the facts straight or they jump to conclusions. I also saw the strength in the South Asian, Muslim and Arab communities and immigrant and people of color communities because they did not take it sitting down. They began organizing.

After 9/11, we saw all of these national policies and how it was affecting our communities in different ways with detentions and deportations and racial profiling. We also saw after, around 2003, that school safety policies changed. They started putting police officers and metal detectors into schools. We did a two year research phase where we conducted 665 surveys with South Asian immigrant students to see how these school policies affected them. Fifty-one percent of them said they had seen or experienced harassment by police officers or school officials. Being exposed to such high levels of harassment doesn't create an environment in which students feel that they can learn. We have to create a school environment that is safe for everyone. Policing a problem is not the same as solving it. Many of the schools that we went to or go to are overcrowded or underfunded, or programs are being cut. This is not how to solve the problem. Actually investing in education—putting in computers and books and smaller class sizes will create a safe environment for everyone.

I Am a Muslim.
I Am Not a Terrorist!

Zebeen Panju

Zebeen Panju is a published writer, a mother, and an entrepreneur. She is a job placement counselor at Douglas College in New Westminster, British Columbia. She writes about the discrimination she and other Muslims have faced in the wake of 9/11. She argues that racial profiling in the name of national security is racist, and she strives to clear up some common misconceptions about Muslims that have been perpetuated by the American media.

Before 9/11, racial profiling was vehemently denied by police, border officers and airport authority. In a 2005 Internet article on CBC News, the author states that, "Some black Canadians have had a name for the practice. When they get pulled over for no reason, they are guilty of "DWB."—driving while black or brown." Since 9/11, racial profiling has become a legitimized way of discriminating against a group because they happen to belong to a particular religion or because they are young, male and Muslim.

My twin sister, Zeineen, and I were exhibitors at a gift show for new entrepreneurs on the day the twin towers fell. As we were driving to BC Place [Stadium], we were shocked at what we heard on the radio and we agreed that if anyone asked us who or what we were we would say "Canadian." On previous days there were curious customers and we were proud to say we were Muslim, but on 9/11, we were more cautious. Some readers may find it difficult to imagine why anyone would ask me or anyone else who or what they are, but it is a question that has been asked of me since coming to

Canada in 1972 from Uganda, East Africa. When asked, "What are you?" I would answer, "I am Canadian." The person would ask again "No, really, what are you?" and when I answered, "I am Muslim, Ismaili Muslim," the answer seemed to satisfy the white face that asked the question. Eventually, I made a conscious effort to explain I am Muslim first then Canadian.

9/11 Changed Everything

In the 70's and 80's racism was the norm for me. I walked knee deep in the stench. Racial names, such as "Paki, Punjab, Turban twister," were slung at me. I was bullied, taunted, harassed, given lousy marks on tests, essays, and passed over for jobs. I even went through a "white-wannabe" stage and during that time, I shunned my people, my culture, my dress, and my ethnic food. Finally, when I turned 23, I looked in the mirror and heard this voice telling me "Girl, you ain't white. You will never be white. Why don't you accept the person you are and be proud of what you are?" After that I embraced my difference and started to enjoy being brown-skinned and Muslim. I ended up marrying a Punjabi Sikh man and had a wonderful daughter. Then 9/11 happened, and the safe, secure, life I had created for myself came tumbling down as the towers crashed. The way I perceived my world changed.

The days following 9/11, I literally hid in my house. I took off the tasbi—our version of the rosary beads—that used to hang proudly around my rearview mirror, so ignorant vandals would not trash my car. I was scared of venturing outside my backyard for fear of stepping on a minefield of hate. Though my life has returned to "normal", the new form of racism that has reared its head in the 21st century is not an easy one to ignore.

Racial Profiling Is Racist

My brother used to travel quite a bit before 9/11 and never had problems. But for months after 9/11, whenever he traveled, he was questioned and his luggage was thoroughly checked. His colleague, who is Asian, was never treated with this type of scrutiny. My brother fits the stereotype—young, male and Muslim. Unfortunately, this narrow-minded focus targets innocent people, as in the case of Maher Arar.

In 1992, Maher Arar, who is a Canadian Citizen, was pulled from a plane in New York while on a stopover from Syria to Montreal. He was accused of being a member of the al Qa'eda terror network and the Americans deported him to Syria because of his dual citizenship. RCMP [Royal Canadian Mounted Police] provided U.S. authorities with "inaccurate intelligence information" that resulted in Arar being put on a "border watch list as a dangerous al-Qa'eda terrorist suspect." While in Syria he was tortured and questioned. He returned to Canada in 2003, and after his story broke and the information about his capture and torture became known, there was a commission inquiry in 2004. In October 2006, he was cleared of all terrorist allegations. His case has proven that racial profiling is discriminatory and racist, and does not work.

Another example of racial profiling happened as recently as November 20, 2006. Six Muslim Imams were handcuffed and removed from a flight at a Minnesota airport and were guilty of nothing more than "flying while Muslim." The pilot of US Airways removed the six men after some passengers reported that the men were "praying loudly" at the airport terminal. Nihad Awad, Council Executive of Council on American-Islamic Relations stated, "We are concerned that crew members, passengers and security personnel may have succumbed to fear and prejudice based on stereotyping of Muslims and Islam." What is so ironic about this incident is the fact that these men were attending a three-day meeting in Minneapolis to discuss "how to build bridges" between Muslims and American society.

Clearing Up Misconceptions

I don't condone for one minute what atrocities are being done in the name of Allah. But I don't accept the ignorance, fear, and blatant acts of discrimination, racism, and oppression that are inflicted upon people, just because they pray to the all mighty Allah. There are many atrocities committed in the name of Christianity, but these are not labeled terrorism like the acts that are allegedly carried out by Muslims. . . .

I am an Ismaili Muslim and follow the Aga Khan, who is our spiritual leader. He is not rich because we give him our money. His wealth is his own. When I pray, I pray to Allah, God, the Universe. My religion, Islam, does not preach hate, killing, or the suppression of women. Our men do not marry more than one wife. That was a century old custom and done at the time of the crusades when men went to war and left their wives behind. A man took more than one wife so she and her offspring were taken care of financially. The real polygamists are in BC, and this practice is alive and well as I write and breathe. I am not on a Jihad. I don't wear a scarf or a hijab. I don't pray five times a day. Hell, I don't even face Mecca when I pray. I don't pray on a carpet, nor do I fly on one. I don't read the Koran every waking moment. I don't own a missile and don't have one buried in my back yard. I don't have a baking pan in the shape of a missile either. I don't own any bomb paraphernalia. The only bombs I make are bath bombs and they explode nicely in my bathtub. I don't wrap my head up in cloth. Sikhs do that and that cloth is called a Turban. I don't carry a knife either. That is a Kirpan and it is worn by Sikhs not Muslims. I am not related to Osama Bin Laden. I make these points to clear up once and for all the misconceptions, questions and queries I have been faced with and have to defend against when I tell someone I am Muslim. My anger is directed towards people who support racial profiling all in the name of national security. It is directed towards policies and acts that are passed in our government condoning racial profiling as a good thing, even though this practice infringes upon our charter rights.

Our government passed an anti-terrorist act (Bills C-36 and C-42), which was Canada's response to combat terrorism, and became part of the Criminal Code on Dec. 18, 2001, but not until after "heated debate and controversy." On October 24, 2006, Justice Douglas Rutherford of Ontario Superior Court "ruled that a section of the Anti-terrorism Act that defines 'terrorism' violates the Charter of Rights and Freedoms." In June 2006 Justice Minister Vic Toews said "There are two problems with [the motive clause] definition: it could lead to profiling of people of a particular religion, Islam."

The Media Distorts the Meaning of Islam

My anger is also directed towards the media and the ones who wield a camera and hold onto a mic and spew their propaganda and misinformation to the public. It is directed towards an elected official who has the gall to commit heinous terrorist attacks against innocent civilians and defends his actions and his nation's action as being a legit fight against terrorism.

What scares me more than anything is the fact that people are being bombarded with distorted images of what Islam is and this new version is what is being ingrained in the minds of millions. The true essence and meaning of Islam, which is about peace, love, knowledge, embracing differences, accepting a pluralistic society, is getting lost because these images are boring and counter to the stereotype of what a terrorist is.

My wish for the future is that my daughter will grow up knowing it is okay to be different and that being a Muslim is a good thing. I also wish when she grows up and someone asks her "What are you?" she will answer "I am Canadian" and it will stop right there.

Hurricane Katrina Was an Unnatural Disaster

Emma Dixon

Emma Dixon lives in Mandeville, Louisiana. She is a financial literacy educator with United for a Fair Economy, a nonpartisan organization concerned about growing income, wage, and wealth inequality in the United States. She describes the institutional racism that developed in the wake of Hurricane Katrina in 2005, one of the nation's deadliest storms that destroyed much of New Orleans. But the "unnatural disaster" of racism was in place long before Katrina came ashore, she says, and this racism only intensified the racist response to the needs of African Americans after the storm.

Persistent institutional racism not only made recovery from Hurricane Katrina more difficult, it created the conditions that allowed the horrors to happen. When Hurricane Katrina tore up the roof of my house, it didn't care that I'm black. My white neighbors, like my black neighbors, saw trees fall on their homes and saw their refrigerators rot and mold. They, like I, lived without electricity or phone for over a week after that color-blind natural disaster.

But an unnatural disaster hit us as well, the institutionalized racism that began centuries ago. The flooded areas of New Orleans were three-quarters black, while in dry areas, African Americans were a minority. Over the years, many well-off white people have left the city for gated suburban communities. The remaining whites tend to live on higher ground.

Racism Hit Before Katrina

The unnatural disaster of racism swept away the savings accounts and credit cards with which poor black people could

Emma Dixon, "Personal Voices: An Unnatural Disaster," AlterNet, November 19, 2005. Reproduced by permission.

have bought their escape. A century of Jim Crow laws barred black families in the South from certain schools and jobs. Social Security benefits were not available at first to domestic and agricultural workers, the occupations of most African Americans at that time. Due to discrimination, most black WWII veterans were unable to use the GI Bill, which gave most white veterans the homeownership and college educations that have made their children and grandchildren so prosperous.

The unnatural disaster of racism swept away the cars with which poor black people could have escaped Katrina. Almost a third of residents of the flooded neighborhoods did not own the cars on which the evacuation plan relied. If the promise to the freed slaves of 40 acres and a mule had been kept, then six generations later, their descendents would own more assets, and the mule would now be a Buick.

Nor has this unnatural disaster abated today, as I learned from my own experience. Almost immediately after Katrina hit my town, I saw spray-painted signs warning that looters would be shot and killed. I was warned by a white neighbor not to move around too much lest I be mistaken as a looter.

We Need Racism Recovery

When my daughter came to get me from my damaged house and drove me to her home in Indiana, we were turned away by a white motel clerk in Illinois on the pretext that there were no vacancies. A later phone call confirmed what their sign said, that rooms were available. I also experienced first-hand racial discrimination in gas lines, and in food and water distribution lines by a police officer.

The world noticed that the evacuees stuck in the Super-Dome and those turned back at gunpoint at the Gretna bridge were mostly black. But who noticed that the first no-bid federal contracts went to white businessmen, cronies of white politicians?

It's hard for me to believe, but this persistent racism is invisible to many white people. A *Time* Magazine poll taken in September [2005] found that while three quarters of blacks believe race and income level played a role in the government response to Hurricane Katrina, only 29 percent of whites felt the same.

The color of money is green, but the color of poverty has a darker hue. Families in the flooded black neighborhoods of New Orleans had a 2004 median income of only $25,759 a year, barely more than half the national average. Why? Louisiana is a low-wage, anti-union state. Many workers have pay so low that they receive public housing and food stamps. New Orleans voters made history by approving a citywide living wage in 2002, but a court blocked it, allowing poverty wages to continue.

Last week I drove home to Louisiana. In my neighborhood I hear the constant buzzing of chain saws removing uprooted trees, and the sounds of hammering as roofers repair endless numbers of damaged roofs. The fragrances of Pine Sol and bleach tinge the air as residents attempt to save refrigerators and rain-soaked carpets. I thank God that my family and I survived the storm, and that the recovery has begun.

Yet I ask myself when the other recovery will begin.

Katrina revealed the racial wealth divide in New Orleans and the unnatural disaster that caused it. When will we rebuild our society so that everyone, regardless of race, has the means to escape the next disaster?

A Report Back from New Orleans

Nzingha Tyehemba

*As a senior at Amherst College in Massachusetts, Nzingha Tye-
hemba was one of the organizers of Project "We Got Your Back-
Pack," an effort to collect school supplies, coloring books, and
other educational materials for distribution to the children and
families impacted by Hurricane Katrina. After visiting New Orleans, she is outraged by the overt racism that led to the disenfranchisement of many people of color in New Orleans. She con-
cludes that colleges such as her own should do more to prevent
institutionalized forms of oppression.*

After a week spent volunteering in New Orleans, I left
overcome with two feelings: one of outrage at the con-
verging influences of racism, classism and capitalism preventing a just rebuilding process, and another of distress at the
way my college delicately skirts challenging these forms of oppression.

I journeyed to New Orleans from Selma, AL with 165
other students, many of whom were African-American and attended historically Black colleges and some who attended historically white ones including Columbia and NYU. As a group,
we constituted the week two participants in a month-long initiative organized by the group Katrina on the Ground to bring
students together with survivors to assist in the rebuilding
process.

In New Orleans, coordinators from the People's Hurricane
Relief Fund and Oversight Coalition integrated us into the
work they had been doing since Katrina hit to provide and
advocate for a just relief and a just return for New Orleanians.

Nzingha Tyehemba, "Report Back from New Orleans," *New York Amsterdam News*, vol.
97, April 27, 2006. Reproduced by permission.

We broke into five groups: gutting and cleaning houses in the Lower Ninth Ward, surveying residents on the streets or at hotels about their needs and desires, conducting exit interviews with recently released prisoners of the Orleans Parish Prison, and helping reestablish a women's health clinic and a community bookstore.

Each night, the majority of our group slept on cots between the pews of the historic St. Augustine's Parish, the oldest Black Catholic Church in the U.S. We arrived just days before the official closing of the parish by the Archdiocese of New Orleans (citing lack of funding) and joined the parishioners in their fight to keep their parish and its many ministries, including a food pantry and clothing drive, open. Father Jerome LeDoux, the African-American priest who has presided at St. Augustine's for the past 15 years, will be replaced by Rev. Michael Jacques, a white pastor from the neighboring St. Peter Claver Parish, whose church, unlike St. Augustine's, was completely devastated by the hurricane. After a thee-week occupation of the church by parishioners and supporters, the Archdiocese granted the parish an eighteen-month reprieve. Father LeDoux will return to the parish, though not as pastor.

At a community meeting held the night before the closing, a parishioner divulged that Archdiocesan officials were in negotiations with Barnes & Noble to present a plan wherein the bookstore giant would "brand" the property of St. Augustine's and the neighborhood of Treme with B&N signs and slogans. Apparently, the two contracting agents could not reach an agreement and the deal fell through. Another parishioner spoke of similar capitalist drives behind the plans for the Lower Ninth Ward. Quite bluntly, the resident said the reason that they, presumably city officials, do not want residents to return is because of the 72 trillion tons of oil purported to be beneath the family houses built there.

While the need for just and comprehensive passages of return for Katrina survivors is ever-present, it appeared to me that city, state, and federal officials have placed more resources in the further displacement and, in regards to New Orleans residents, disenfranchisement of Katrina survivors.

For instance, prior to Hurricane Katrina, Blacks, Latinos and a small Vietnamese population inhabited Village Square, a small neighborhood in the overwhelmingly white parish of St. Bernard's. Lynn Dean, a white St. Bernard Parish resident of over fifty years and member of his parish's governing council, is the sole vocal opponent of his council's decision to demolish Village Square. According to Dean, his council's contention that the Square is prone to flooding is unjustifiable. He demonstrated on a map indicating flood-prone areas in the parish that Village Square is the least likely of places to flood in the whole of the parish.

Dean said that the council of seven plans to build condominiums and possibly a golf course in Village Square. However, debris removal, demolition and other projects in the parish have come to a standstill, Dean explained, as FEMA [Federal Emergency Management Agency] will not give the council any more funding until it can account for $30 million—$10 million of which the council cannot produce receipts for.

Another instance of a continual slapping in the face of the city's residents, many of whom are Black and poor, is the situation with public housing. On our way to Tulane University to shower, we passed a development of two-story brick buildings, collectively known as The Projects, whose doors and windows had been sealed shut with steel plates. In another development, a barbed wire fence had been constructed around the buildings blocking access to returning residents.

As I said at the start of this piece, I returned home to Harlem with my senses sharpened to the injurious way endemic forms of oppressions continue to infiltrate people's lives. My thoughts drifted to Amherst [College] and the colorful catalogues, diversity orientations, special diversity weekends and other diversity initiatives common on campus. I asked myself, was Amherst really working to reenergize its efforts to take on the various forms of oppression that serve as stumbling blocks to any true progress, or, was the school, like other colleges and universities, operating behind a facade?

Instead of circumventing the work needed to eradicate institutionalized forms of oppression, college administration, faculty and students must confront the systems of power and privilege that we as individuals and together as an institution foster. In doing so, we will leave this college better equipped to deal with the world's inability to eradicate, let alone dialogue about, race, sex, class, etc.

I believe educational institutions have a certain responsibility to take up this cause in a more than half-hearted way because of their self-imposed charge to prepare their students for the world. What I would suggest as one way for Amherst to reintegrate itself into the politics of this country would be to institutionalize an anti-oppression curriculum, such as the in-service learning program that I participated in over Spring Break. As students we might graduate willing or at least able to, as our motto advises, give light to the world.

My Thoughts on Virginia Tech

Tricia Wang

Tricia Wang is a PhD candidate and instructor in sociology at the University of California, San Diego. After Korean student Seung-Hui Cho killed thirty-two students and professors at Virginia Polytechnic Institute and State University on April 16, 2007, Wang is upset that Asian students on her campus are too focused on the Asian connection to the shooting. Wang argues that in the wake of the tragedy people should be more focused on gun control and other public policies than on the potential for racial backlash against other Asians. She encourages Asian advocacy groups to expand their efforts to embrace all minorities, and not just their own causes.

I was walking to teach my section today when a student approached me and asked if I would like to sign a banner that would be sent to the students at Virginia Tech [Virginia Polytechnic Institute and State University]. I looked it over—and it was organized by the Korean American Students Association at UC [University of California] San Diego.

I asked the student why I should sign it and how that would support Virginia Tech, and he said "well I'm Asian and you're Asian—and we need to support the students."

I asked "what does that have to do with being Asian" and he said "we also need to fight racism against Asians—since the shooter was Korean."

When I glanced at the banner again, I realized the 20 students signing this Korean Association Banner for Virginia Tech were all Asian. I took a picture and walked away. Then one of the Korean Student Assoc. girls yelled out—"instead of taking a picture you should sign our banner."

Tricia Wang, "My Thoughts on Virginia Tech, Asians, Condolences, Racism, and etc.," triciawang.vox.com, April 17, 2007. Reproduced by permission.

As I watched from afar, I noticed that the student who was asking students to sign the banner was only approaching Asian students for signing their banner. Although Asians are the ethno-racial majority on campus, there were plenty of white students around and he didn't ask any of them within the 5 minutes of my observation.

Some Things Are More Pressing than Racism

I walked away very upset at what just happened. I felt it was so petty to worry about Asian racism (they did it by cloaking it in "we're concerned for students at Virginia Tech)" when this horrific tragedy just happened!

Why is it that this Virginia Tech shooting prompted this Asian Club to address racism—when really there are more immediate issues that this shooting has brought up—like gun control policy, identifying psychological maniacs on the verge of massacring others, emergency planning, effective campus security, and emotional reverberations around other college campuses?

And then immediately I thought of the e-mail that Liane just sent me—it was a press release post from the Asian American Journalists Association, urging the media to refrain from using racial identifiers of "Asian" or "Korean" in reference to the shooter. "There is no evidence at this early point that the race or ethnicity of the suspected gunman has anything to do with the incident, and to include such mention serves only to unfairly portray an entire people. The effect of mentioning race can be powerfully harmful. It can subject people to unfair treatment based simply on skin color and heritage," said the release.

This press release made me very upset, not because of what they are urging (which is a great idea but a bit too late). First of all racism is not the immediate concern in this situation. What I am most upset about is that the Asian American

Journalists are only expressing concern for this specific situation because they fear that they themselves will face epiphenomenonic racism. They wouldn't have spoken up if the shooter were white or Black. Although there is nothing wrong with being concerned about the potential racism one will face, as it will also upset me when the stereotype of "Angry Asian Man Gone Wild" develops . . . what's wrong is that they only choose to speak up when it became a fear that Asians themselves would face discrimination because of the shooting.

Asian Groups Only Advocate for Asians

This is one of the reasons why I find it difficult to work with Asian-American non-profit organizations or collectives that create spaces for equality and community—because ultimately it is too often that Asian activists who fight against discrimination and for representation, are only fighting for Asians. They forget that their are other minorities that are fighting for the same causes, and that building coalitions and solidarity with Blacks, Latinos, Queers, Jews and other minorities—is a more powerful strategy to fight for equality.

Jewish, Black and Latino organizations are always fighting discrimination when it happens to an individual or group other than themselves. They really take on Martin Luther King's quote—that "injustice anywhere is is a threat to justice everywhere." But Asian organizations don't speak up enough when discrimination happens to another group other than themselves. . . .

What Asian groups need to realize, is that if they are really fighting racism/discrimination, then they need to fight equally for all races/ethnicities—otherwise they're just favoring one race/group when they are fighting—themselves. They speak up when they become worried that they, as Asians, may face similar forms of discrimination that Blacks, Latinos, Jews and anyone else who is dark has had or continues to experience— especially in the aftermath of a highly public shooting/

massacres/murders. Where were Asian groups during post 9–11 Muslim/anyone-wearing-a-turban/dark colored person discrimination period? Where were they when Matthew Shepard was killed for being gay? Or for the Amadou Diallo shooting?

Asians Can Honor Asians and Others Equally

This is not the case for all Asian individuals or organizations in America—I am reflecting on what I have noticed as a community organizer and media researcher. I am sure there are individuals and organizations who do speak up, but nationally Asian groups have not made a great media impact when fighting for others—at least nothing comparable to the effort they are now putting into fighting potential racism against Asians in the face of Virginia Tech.

The Yellow Debris of the Virginia Tech Shootings

Angela J. Lee

Angela J. Lee is a Korean American graduate student in English at California Polytechnic University in Pomona, and is currently an Editor for KASTN *(Korean-American Science and Technology News). Lee is dismayed that fellow Korean, Seung-Hui Cho, was responsible for killing thirty-two people at Virginia Polytechnic Institute and State University in April 2007. She regrets that other Koreans did not reach out to Cho, who was obviously a disturbed and isolated person. Lee also worries that the media focus on Cho's race will have a negative impact on the Korean American community. She encourages Korean Americans not to detach themselves from the shooting, but to support each other and strive to make their community a better place for future generations.*

It has been ten days since the deadliest shooting [on April 16, 2007] at Virginia Tech [Virginia Polytechnic Institute and State University]. I am no longer bombarded with images of a cold-blooded killer who looks just like me, and I no longer feel the need to frantically google Seung Hui Cho or Virginia Tech shooting in order to get the latest news on the investigation. My professors no longer bring it up in class and I no longer feel the need to "prepare" myself for possible discussions that may arise in our English graduate seminars, as the only Korean in a room full of Caucasian students. I am no longer angry at the media for continuously labeling the shooter as "South Korean immigrant," and calling him Cho Seung Hui instead of Seung Hui Cho. I am no longer analyzing and critiquing every movement made by the mainstream

Angela J. Lee, "The Yellow Debris of the Virginia Tech Shooting," *KASTN: Korean-American Science and Technology News*, May 23, 2007. Reproduced by permission.

media to make sure that they're not fueling more racial tension and anxiety. I remember the Rodney King beating and the L.A. Riot all too clearly. And I don't ever want to see our Korean American community go through something like that ever again.

So now, ten days later, the initial shock and horror caused by this incident are slowly dying down, and mainstream America seems fairly convinced that this shooting was simply an act of one crazy individual who "happened" to be Asian. Many people seem to agree that we, as Korean Americans, should not feel the need to apologize for what happened at Virginia Tech because we're not like Seung Hui. We're not crazy and we're not a "cold-blooded murderer." He is just one kid gone bad, one black sheep amongst thousands of hardworking, extremely driven, highly intellectual Korean Americans who continue to live up to their image of the "model-minority," right?

Lots of Questions Remain

But why is it that I can't seem to shake off Seung Hui's face out of my mind? Why do I find myself constantly wondering and questioning, with a frail hope that I can make some sense of what happened at Virginia Tech that day? How could he have done what he did? Why? For whom?

While mainstream America sees the face of a cold-blooded killer in what they call his "multimedia manifesto," I can't help but to see the loner Korean kid who always sat quietly in the back of the classroom, whom everyone ignored, including me. While others see nothing but images of extreme disturbance and violence in his final pictures, I can't help but to see a sickened and tortured soul who was somehow led to believe that he had no reason to live, and absolutely nothing to lose. While other Korean parents purposely take their children out of the house so their children do not have to see such disturbing images of another Korean, I can't help but to wish that my daughters were old enough to understand what just happened, so they can start making a difference.

We, as Korean Americans, understand the struggles we face while living in America as immigrants. Yes we're known as "model-minorities," and many of us do make great doctors, lawyers, engineers, etc., but behind this positive facade, often lie lonely, confused, segregated, and deeply wounded individuals who struggle between their conflicting lives at home and at school. I, too, am guilty of being too caught up with my own pursuit of happiness and success, that I failed to gain the courage or to recognize the need to reach out to these silenced individuals around me. Or perhaps I never fully understood just how much these people were hurting inside.

America Is Not Color-Blind

In an ideal, Utopian society, every single person in this country (regardless of their color) would have seen a cold-blooded, psychotic mass murderer on TV, not an Asian one. They would have seen Seung Hui simply as an extremely disturbed and troubled kid who just spun out of control without mentioning his race at all. But in reality, the fact that Seung Hui was a "South Korean immigrant" was plastered all over the media, and his foreign name can't be expected to be taken by mainstream America as "John" or "Bob"—although we can't blame them for making racial distinctions that clearly exist. Moreover, no matter how hard we try to gain racial equality in our society, we can't escape the fact that we'll always be marginalized as minorities. No matter how "Americanized" we are, we can't help but to feel right at home when we're surrounded by other Koreans or Asians. We can try to detach ourselves all we want from the Virginia Tech shooting in disgust and shame, but we can't assume that the white man who lives somewhere in the Midwest won't recall the face of Seung Hui when he runs into another yellow face with slanted eyes. If you feel that we live in a "color-blind" society, I would ask you to look around our Asian neighbors, say, Chinese Americans. The first Chinese entered California in the 1800's and even now, a few hundred years later in 2007, they are still considered a minority. The Japanese American community consists of Issei, Nisei, and even Sansei generations but they, too, are still marginalized by the dominant white society.

My point here is this. Let's not try to detach ourselves from this incident and foolishly think that it does not affect us because it does. This incident may not change things for you with your White co-worker, or with the Black student who you sit next to in class; but let's keep in mind that somewhere out there in this country, there will always be that lonely, segregated, and neglected individual who is constantly struggling to find a place in our society. There will always be that oppressed and isolated Korean boy, who faces teasing at school, only to come home to parents who demand a 1600 SAT score and a 4.0 GPA. There will always be that emotionally and mentally destroyed Korean girl, who grew up in a dysfunctional home with an alcoholic father who beat her mother. There will always be that silenced Korean girl who does not know how to tell her parents that she was sexually molested by her neighbor or boss, because she's afraid of causing them so much shame.

Cho's Plays Are Alarming

Although I claim that I'm no longer upset at the media for their portrayal of Seung Hui, I *am* keenly aware of the deliberate editing strategies employed by them for their own benefits (or perhaps to pacify mainstream white America). For example, they completely overlook the fact that his writings were not simply that of "macabre" violence, but rather, of being a victim of sexual violence. Instead of noting that the boy is victimized in both his plays, the media only quotes parts of the play that depicts him as the perpetrator. I do not intend to make any claims that I cannot justify, but I am unable to understand how such well-respected, award-winning English professors could have overlooked the source of "real" violence of his plays. Did they not see that his writings were about an angry kid who is sexually molested by his stepfather, and about a kid who is "ass-raped" by a teacher who "won't leave him alone?" Did they not see that both plays end by the boy being victimized—by getting struck by his stepfather and robbed by his teacher? As a graduate student of English studies, I do not understand how trained literary scholars can overlook something so alarming. Quite frankly, I'm not convinced that his professors were really just trying to "help." I imagine that they simply wanted him out of their classes, with the same attitude of other students who passed by him on campus daily without saying a word to him. He was weird. He was crazy. He didn't talk. And that was that. They just left him alone to immerse himself even deeper in his grief that eventually led to insanity and violence. Due to one individual's repressed anger and ignored outcries, thirty-two students' [and teachers'] innocent lives were taken away abruptly, and this incident will now be remembered as the bloodiest school shooting in US history.

Koreans Need to Reach Out to Each Other

I do not want to give an impression that I'm justifying Seung Hui's killings because I'm not. There is no way I can overlook the fact that 32 innocent students [and teachers] were killed. And yes, what he did was truly wrong and unthinkable. And yes, not every "disturbed" kid kills 32 [people] before killing himself. And yes, many Korean Americans grow up in dysfunctional homes and do not necessarily turn out to be a cold-blooded murderer. But as I said earlier, this is no longer about me, you, or your immediate family and friends. This is about those in our community—our brothers, sisters, cousin, parents, grandparents, and more importantly, our children and their children—to prevent something like this from ever happening again. Instead of turning our backs in shame or disgust at the atrocious crime committed by a fellow Korean, and calling ourselves to be more American than Korean, we have to recognize the urgency to reach out to others in our community and further, repair some of the damages caused by our previous generation. I understand the hardships of immigrant life all too well because, I, like many of you, have lived it. I saw, firsthand, how hard-working, diligent, honest, and strong our parents can be. But on the other hand, I saw many Korean Americans struggling to bridge the gap between two conflicting cultures by trying to assimilate into the American society, while still fulfilling our parents' very "Korean" expectations. I also witnessed many Korean parents turning the other way, and simply refusing to believe the harsh realities of their children's lives due to feelings of shame, disgrace, and perhaps, filial duty to their mother country. No matter what the reason is, this is a time for us to re-examine, re-explore, and re-think about our roles in our American society, as well as our duty to our Korean community. It took 33 lives [Cho killed himself after killing thirty-two people] for us to finally realize the tears shed and cries unanswered behind closed doors of many Korean immigrants' homes. We can no longer look away from their tears. We can no longer hide from their outcries. This is a time for us to open our eyes, our ears, and our hearts to those around us, so the 33 tragic deaths do not go to waste. By condemning the shooter in anger and hatred, we're simply fueling another mentally-disturbed and neglected individual to consider dying the same death.

I'm not American. I'm not Korean. I'm Korean-American and this hyphenated identity brings me so much pride, strength, and self-awareness. And I ask that you let go of your anger, join hands with our brothers and sisters, and step onto this journey to empower ourselves and our community to make America a better place for future generations of Korean Americans.

Organizations to Contact

The editors have compiled the following list of organizations concerned with the issues debated in this book. The descriptions are derived from materials provided by the organizations. All have publications or information available for interested readers. The list was compiled on the date of publication of the present volume; the information provided here may change. Be aware that many organizations take several weeks or longer to respond to inquiries, so allow as much time as possible.

American Civil Liberties Union (ACLU)
125 Broad St., Eighteenth Floor, New York, NY 10004
(212) 549-2500
e-mail: aclu@aclu.org
Web site: www.aclu.org

The ACLU is a national organization that works to defend Americans' civil rights as guaranteed by the U.S. Constitution. It provides legal defense, research, and education. The ACLU publishes and distributes policy statements, pamphlets, and an online newsletter available by subscription.

Intermix
PO Box 29441, London NW1 8FZ
   United Kingdom
0207-485-2869
e-mail: contact@intermix.org.uk
Web site: www.intermix.org.uk

Intermix is an organization based in the United Kingdom with the goal of uniting people of all races and promoting increased racial understanding. Intermix is a nonprofit organization that focuses mainly on providing information about mixed-race individuals and families. It offers an extensive database of varying media on the topic of mixed-race and publishes a monthly newsletter.

Interracial Voice (IV)
PO Box 560185, College Point, NY   11356
(718) 909-1878
e-mail: intvoice@webcom.com
Web site: www.webcom.com/~intvoice

IV is a group that provides information about multiracial issues and offers individuals an opportunity to voice their opinions about these topics. The organization's Web site contains many links to multiracial resources including other sites, news articles, and census information.

MAVIN Foundation
600 First Ave., Suite 600, Seattle, WA   98104
(206) 622-7101 • fax: (206) 622-2231
e-mail: info@mavinfoundation.org
Web site: www.mavinfoundation.org

The MAVIN Foundation is a cultural identity support group that encourages individuals to connect with their racial and ethnic background. The ultimate goal is to redefine the culture of racial and ethnic heritage in the United States and reject old notions of race. The organization publishes the magazine *MAVIN* and other books, pamphlets, and educational materials. It also offers a student internship program.

Multicultural Council of Saskatchewan (MCoS)
369 Part St., Regina   SK S4N 5B2
   Canada
(306) 721-2767 • fax: (306) 721-3342
e-mail: mcos@accesscomm.ca
Web site: http://mcos.sask.com

MCoS promotes positive cross-cultural relations and the recognition of cultural diversity. Its publications include *Faces Magazine* and *Multiculturalisrn Matters*. MCoS also distributes information concerning multiculturalism, such as multifaith calendars, to the public.

Multiethnic Education Program (ME Program)
1581 Le Roy Ave, Berkeley, CA   94708
(510) 644-1000 • fax: (510) 525-4106
Web site: www.multiethniceducation.org

The ME Program promotes new attitudes toward multiethnic education for children. It offers training, education, and educational resources for individuals involved in education and child-care fields as well as for students.

National Urban League
120 Wall St., New York, NY   10005
(212) 558-5600 • fax: (212) 344-5332
e-mail: info@nul.org
Web site www.nul.org

A community service agency, the National Urban League aims to eliminate institutional racism in the United States. It also provides services for minorities who experience discrimination in employment, housing, welfare, and other areas. It publishes numerous journals and studies on diversity issues and the black American experience.

New Demographic
244 Fifth Ave, Suite J230, New York, NY   10001
(917) 657-3886
e-mail: team@newdemographic.com
Web site: www.newdemographic.com

New Demographic is a diversity training firm codirected by Jen Chau and Carmen Van Kerckhove. In addition to workshops that offer new perspectives on multiracial topics, the organization publishes a monthly newsletter available on its Web site. New Demographic also cohosts the biweekly podcast radio show *Addicted to Race* about race in America and coedits *Mixed Media Watch,* an online Web log that provides posts on representations of multiracial families and individuals in the media.

Project RACE
PO Box 2366, Los Banos, CA   93635 •fax: (209) 826-2510
e-mail: projrac@aol.com
Web site: www.projectrace.com

Project RACE is an advocacy group that promotes new methods for racial classification on all forms that request racial data. One branch of the group is Teen Project RACE which allows teenagers to have a voice in multiracial issues.

Sojourners
3333 Fourteenth St. NW, Suite 200, Washington, DC   20010
(202) 328-8842 • fax: (202) 328-8757
e-mail: sojourners@sojo.net
Web site: www.sojourners.com

Sojourners is an ecumenical Christian organization committed to racial justice and reconciliation between races. It publishes *America's Original Sin* as well as the monthly *Sojourners* magazine.

Tolerance.org
c/o The Southern Poverty Law Center
400 Washington Ave., Montgomery, AL   36104
(334) 956-8200 • fax: (334) 956-8488
Web site: www.tolerance.org

Tolerance.org is an online group that provides information about increasing diversity and breaking down hate and racial barriers. It provides both online resources and print materials for children, teens, parents, and educators. There is a bimonthly online newsletter available by subscription and free classroom resources for teachers. The group receives support from the Southern Poverty Law Center.

United States Commission on Civil Rights
624 Ninth St. NW, Washington, DC   20425
(202) 376-7700
Web site: www.usccr.gov

A fact-finding body, the United States Commission on Civil Rights reports directly to Congress and the president on the effectiveness of equal opportunity programs and laws. A catalog of its numerous publications can be obtained from its Web site.

For Further Research

Books

Kimberly Battle-Walters, *Sheila's Shop: Working Class African American Women Talk Life, Love, Race, and Hair.* Lanham, MD: Rowman & Littlefield, 2004.

Kenneth Bolton, *Black in Blue: African-American Police Officers and Racism.* New York: Routledge, 2004.

Cynthia Carr, *Our Town: A Heartland Lynching, a Haunted Town, and the History of White America.* New York: Crown, 2006.

Pyong Gap, *Encyclopedia of Racism in the United States.* Westport, CT: Greenwood, 2005.

Robert Gooding-Williams, *Look! A Negro!: Philosophical Essays on Race, Culture, and Politics.* New York: Routledge, 2006.

Steve Holbert, *The Color of Guilt and Innocence: Racial Profiling and Practices in America.* San Ramon, CA: Page Marque, 2004.

Gary R. Howard, *We Can't Teach What We Don't Know: White Teachers, Multiracial Schools.* New York: Teacher's College Press, 1999.

Elliot Jaspin, *Buried in the Bitter Waters: The Hidden History of Racial Cleansing in America.* New York: Basic Books, 2007.

Jack Levin, *The Violence of Hate: Confronting Racism, Anti-Semitism, and Other Forms of Bigotry.* Boston: Pearson, 2007.

Curtis Linton, *Courageous Conversations About Race: A Field Guide for Equity in Schools.* Thousand Oaks, CA: Corwin, 2006.

Sherry Marx, *Revealing the Invisible: Confronting Passive Racism in Teacher Education.* New York: Routledge, 2006.

Dwight A. McBride, *Why I Hate Abercrombie & Fitch: Essays on Race and Sexuality.* New York: New York University Press, 2005.

Karyn D. McKinney, *Being White: Stories of Race and Racism.* New York: Routledge, 2005.

Kristen A. Myers, *Racetalk: Racism Hiding in Plain Sight.* Lanham, MD: Rowman & Littlefield, 2006.

Barack Obama, *Dreams of My Father: A Story of Race and Inheritance.* Kent, OH: Kent State University Press, 2004.

Mudita Rastogi, *Voices of Color: First Person Accounts of Ethnic Minority Therapists.* Thousand Oaks, CA: Sage, 2005.

Ali Rattansi, *Racism: A Very Short Introduction.* New York: Oxford University Press, 2007.

Katheryn Russell-Brown, *Protecting Our Own: Race, Crime, and African Americans.* Lanham, MD: Rowman & Littlefield, 2006.

Todd Lee Savitt, *Race and Medicine in Nineteenth- and Early-Twentieth-Century America.* Kent, OH: Kent State University Press, 2007.

Nikhil Pal Singh, *Black Is a Country: Race and the Unfinished Struggle for Democracy.* Cambridge, MA: Harvard University Press, 2004.

Dennis Watlington, *Chasing America: Notes from a Rock 'n' Soul Integrationist.* New York: St. Martin's, 2006.

Juan Williams, *My Soul Looks Back in Wonder: Voices of the Civil Rights Experience.* New York: AARP, 2004.

Mary Williams, *Racism.* San Diego: Greenhaven, 2004.

Periodicals

Nado Aveling, "Anti-Racism in Schools: A Question of Leadership?" *Discourse: Studies in the Cultural Politics of Education*, March 2007.

Moustafa Bayoumi, "Arab America's September 11," *Nation*, September 25, 2006.

Michael Cieply, "Films with Black Stars Seek to Break International Barriers," *New York Times*, February 28, 2007.

Allison Dorsey, "Black History Is American History: Teaching African American History in the Twenty-First Century," *Journal of American History*, March 2007.

Anne Gray, "The War on Terror's Impact on the Community," *Race & Class*, April–June 2007.

Heather A. Harding, "'City Girl': A Portrait of a Successful White Urban Teacher," *Qualitative Inquiry*, February 2005.

C. Richard King, "White Power and Sport," *Journal of Sport & Social Issues*, February 2007.

Bruce Kluger, "Racism: What Do We Tell the Kids?" *USA Today*, February 21, 2007.

Jenny Lee, "Welcome to America? International Student Perceptions of Discrimination," *Higher Education*, March 2007.

Alton H. Maddox Jr., "Racism and the Virginia Tech Massacre," *New York Amsterdam News*, April 26, 2007.

Luis Mirón, "Drowning the Crescent City: Told Stories of Katrina," *Cultural Studies/Critical Methodologies*, May 2007.

New Statesman, "What Did Rock Against Racism Mean to You?" April 23, 2007.

Laura Parker, "A Jury's Stand Against Racism Reflects Hope for Change," *USA Today*, April 26, 2007.

Bree Picower, "Teaching Outside One's Race," *Radical Teacher*, September 2004.

Scott Poynting, "The Resistible Rise of Islamophobia," *Journal of Sociology*, March 2007.

Sangeeta Ray, "Crash or How White Men Save the Day, Again," *College English*, March 2007.

Kelefa Sanneh, "Don't Blame Hip-Hop," *New York Times*, April 25, 2007.

Rudy Sayres, "Pros and Cons: Americanism Against Islamism in the 'War on Terror,'" *Muslim World*, January 2007.

Alan Schwarz, "Study of N.B.A. Sees Racial Bias in Calling Fouls," *New York Times*, May 2, 2007.

Stephanie Sellers, "The Experience of a Native American English Professor in Central Pennsylvania," *American Indian Quarterly*, Winter–Spring 2003.

Ericka Sóuter, "Poisoned Water: Negligence or Racism?" *People*, May 14, 2007.

Brian Steinberg, "Facing Ad Defection, NBC Takes Don Imus Show off TV," *Wall Street Journal*, April 12, 2007.

Shirley Tate, "Black Beauty: Shade, Hair and Anti-Racist Aesthetics," *Ethnic & Racial Studies*, March 2007.

Cathy Young, "No, This Is the Story of the Hurricane," *Reason*, December 2005.

Index

A

African Americans
  obsession with race among, 29
  racism against blacks among, personal narrative on coming to terms with, 24–29
  self-segregation by, 60–61
American Indian Quarterly (magazine), 12
Anderson, Danica, 21–22
Arar, Maher, 77
Awad, Nihad, 77

B

Bigotry, difficulty in admitting to, 26, 29
Blacks. *See* African Americans
Boston Globe (newspaper), 13

C

Carson, Essence, 41
Carter, Duncan, 15
Class conflict, racial warfare vs., 28
Colleges/universities
  racial self-segregation on, 60–61
  racism in graduate school, personal narrative on, 62–69

D

Dean, Lynn, 85

E

Ebonics, controversy over, 48–49

F

Foreign travel, as positive experience, 33–34

G

Gradin, Sherrie, 15

H

hooks, bell, 14–15
Hurricane Katrina
  institutional racism and, 80–82
  recovery from, displacement of minorities in, 84–85

I

Imus, Don, 13–14
  response of Rutgers's Scarlet Knights to insults by, 35–43
Islam, media distorts meaning of, 79

J

Jackson, Jesse, 43
Japan, attitudes toward foreigners in, 31

K

Katrina. *See* Hurricane Katrina

L

LeDoux, Jerome, 84

M

Martin, Rose, 50
McKenna, Tom, 12